MODERN *Crochet* SWEATERS

20 Chic Designs for Everyday Wear

JANINE MYSKA
Creator of Knits 'N Knots

PAGE STREET
PUBLISHING CO.

PAGE STREET
PUBLISHING CO.

Copyright © 2021 Janine Myska

First published in 2021 by
Page Street Publishing Co.
27 Congress Street, Suite 105
Salem, MA 01970
www.pagestreetpublishing.com

Distributed by Macmillan, sales in Canada by The Canadian Manda Group.

25   24   23   22   21   1   2   3   4   5

ISBN-13: 978-1-64567-378-1
ISBN-10: 1-64567-378-2

Library of Congress Control Number: 2021931367

Cover and book design by Kylie Alexander for Page Street Publishing Co.
Photography by Stephanie Lauren

Printed and bound in China

To anyone who has shared my work, bought my patterns, or made my designs.

I get to wake up and do what I love every day, and to you I'll always be grateful.

Contents

Introduction

Growing up in Winnipeg, I've experienced my fair share of harsh, cold winters. It wasn't until I learned to knit and crochet in 2016 that I really began to find beauty in the winter season. Nothing beats the magical way the snow gently covers the trees after a fresh snowfall, or the feeling of gratefulness that comes from experiencing a blizzard from the comfort of your warm home. Spending most of the year designing cool-weather garments has given me a reason to look forward to and appreciate the beauty of the cooler months, and that appreciation began when I started viewing autumn and winter as sweater weather season—the time of the year that welcomed handmade sweaters, allowing me to proudly wear all my designs.

While I wholeheartedly love both knitting and crocheting, I was drawn to the artistic freedom that comes with crochet, and I fall more in love with crocheting with every passing year. Learning to crochet didn't just teach me how to turn yarn into fabric, it unlocked a part of my mind that I didn't know existed and opened a whole realm of aesthetic possibilities for me; creating wearable art. Crocheting inspired me to experiment with other art forms and infuse more creativity into my daily life. Crochet is more than just a craft, it's a form of self-expression—a way of transforming ideas into something tangible you can experience, teaching you to appreciate the process of building something slowly with intention. As soon as I explored the limitless world of pattern design, I knew I had to integrate pattern-writing into my daily life. I didn't expect to love it so much that I would drop my master's program and design patterns for a living, but this fiber journey has been my life's most wonderful surprise.

Today, crochet is all about reinventing old techniques in fresh new designs. Most people think of granny squares and doilies when they hear the word "crochet," and while this may have been accurate years ago, today, crochet is infinitely versatile. This collection of patterns proves that modern, youthful garments can be created without advanced techniques or complicated stitchwork. I wanted to demonstrate how easy it is to create beautiful pieces of clothing using only fundamental, basic stitches that anyone can master.

When I explored the idea of writing a book, I knew I had to stick with what I knew best—a size-inclusive collection of simple crochet sweaters that you'll actually want to wear. What I ended up creating is a book filled with wearable patterns that are curated with style, fit and comfort in mind. They say that classic fashion marries comfort and style without compromising on either, and that was my philosophy when designing these sweaters. Each design is subtle and understated, allowing the beauty of the piece to shine through without too many distractions. These designs are chic, everyday pieces with uncomplicated stitch patterns that can be dressed up or down to blend seamlessly with items you already own.

Like all of my designs, each pattern is written to suit a range of bodies, for sizes XS through 5X. Beautifully fitting sweaters are for everybody, and I want you to feel as though this book was written just for you. Use any of these designs as a base to let your creativity run wild: Experiment with fibers, play with color and infuse your own personality into each pattern. It is my honor to play a small part in your creative journey and provide you with a blueprint to create something meaningful. You'll find customization tips within each pattern to help you achieve the best possible fit for your unique body measurements.

This collection of patterns was written for the crocheter who has experience with following written crochet patterns, maybe even some experience with garment-making, and is ready to further explore crocheting your own clothes. Intended to keep your interest without being attention-demanding, most of these patterns are mindless and meditative, requiring little attention to the instructions once the stitch pattern is established, and most can be completed within a week in any size. Once you are familiar with the basic techniques, you'll find these sweaters are achievable, fun and addictive.

Let me show you how simple stitches can create infinitely modern designs. I can't wait to see your unique versions of these patterns! Make sure to tag me on Instagram @knitsnknotswpg and use the hashtag #ModernCrochetSweaters so I can see your work!

Getting Started

Pattern Notes

Unless otherwise indicated, the following notes apply to all patterns:

Right-Handed vs Left-Handed Crocheters: The pattern is written with right-handed crocheters in mind (those who hold their hook in their right hand and crochet each row toward the left). If you are a left-handed crocheter, any instructions referring to the "right-hand side" or "left-hand side" should be reversed.

Sizing: Each sweater is written in nine sizes as follows: XS (S, M, L, XL) (2X, 3X, 4X, 5X). Make sure to follow the numbers for your size only. If you need some help with reading patterns, turn to the section at the back called A Beginner's Guide to Reading Patterns (page 166).

Seaming: When seaming sleeves onto your garment, make sure to keep this seam loose and do not pull tight in order to maintain some stretch; otherwise, this seam will restrict your arms during wear.

Turning Chain: The turning chain does not count as a stitch.

Stitch Counts: Stitch counts are listed after each row or round. If no stitch count is given, there has been no change since the previous row/round. If only one number is provided, it applies to all sizes.

Reversible: There is no right side or wrong side; both sides are identical. You choose which side to wear as the "right side."

Sleeves: For any of the patterns that feature seamed sleeves in this book, if you think the measurements of a different size would better suit your arm measurements, you can follow the instructions for any sleeve size; you don't necessarily have to stick with the same size you have been working up to this point if you think another size will give you a better fit.

Project Difficulty Levels

Although none of these patterns involve any intricate or complicated stitchwork, I have included difficulty levels for each pattern based on the techniques involved in creating that piece. This book follows the standards of the Craft Yarn Council in its sizing and pattern instructions.

There are three levels of difficulty in this book:

Basic: This designation is suitable for crocheters who know how to read and follow a pattern but may not have crocheted a garment. My Silent Night Velvet Cardigan (page 93) and Wandering Willow Faux Fur Capelet (page 71) are designated as basic and are suitable for crocheters easing their way into garment-making.

Easy: Most patterns in this book fall under this category.

Intermediate: There are four patterns in this book designated as intermediate because they involve short rows and some more advanced shaping.

Finding Your Perfect Fit

How Do I Know What Size to Make?

This book follows the industry-leading sizing standards as outlined by the Craft Yarn Council.

Most knit and crochet patterns use the Craft Yarn Council as a resource to standardize knit and crochet terminology and sizing. Their website (craftyarncouncil.com) includes valuable information on everything from standard abbreviations; hook sizes; body sizes for men, women and children and so much more. You can visit craftyarncouncil.com/standards/woman-size to view their detailed sizing chart to help determine which size your measurements fall under. The patterns in this book include a sizing chart to help you decide which size to make, but it can be helpful to get an understanding of where you usually fall within standard crochet sizing.

Each pattern in this book is accompanied by a sizing chart and schematic, detailing the measurements as well as the intended ease for the pattern. Ease refers to the difference between the size of a finished garment and the size of your body. For example, if you have a 40-inch (102-cm) bust, and a garment has a finished bust circumference of 46 inches (117 cm), this means the garment has 6 inches (15 cm) of positive ease, or measures 6 inches (15 cm) larger than your actual bust circumference. Similarly, a garment can have negative ease, meaning it measures smaller than your body for a tight fit. In this book, sometimes the ease differs from size to size within the same pattern, with more positive ease for the smaller sizes, and less ease for the plus sizes. This is usually done on oversized pieces to help give all sizes the best possible fit.

Of course, measurements also differ between people within the same size bracket. You can take a dozen people who all fall under the size "medium," and they will all differ slightly in their body measurements because people have different proportions and distribute weight differently. That is the great thing about making your own clothes—you can tailor them to suit your unique body measurements. The sweaters in this book include instructions on how to adjust the pattern if your body measurements differ from those provided in the sizing chart. Following the pattern exactly will likely yield a great-fitting sweater no matter what, but the helpful tips included along the way will allow you to alter the pattern slightly if you feel you need any adjustments for an even better fit.

How to Correctly Measure Different Parts of Your Body

For just about every design in this book, you will need to know the measurement of your bust, upper arm and wrist. A few designs require you to know the measurement of your waist and hips.

To get the most accurate measurement, make sure the tape measure is held taught against your body.

When measuring the bust, hold the measuring tape around the circumference of the widest part of your chest. Measure over any undergarments you plan to wear under your sweater. If you will wear a bra and tank top under your sweater, measure yourself while wearing a bra and tank top.

When measuring the upper arm, hold the measuring tape around the circumference of the widest part of your bicep.

When measuring the wrist, hold the measuring tape around the circumference of your wrist at the wristbone.

When measuring the waist, hold the measuring tape around the circumference of the smallest part of your waist, usually around the belly button.

When measuring the hips, hold the measuring tape around the circumference of the widest part of your hips.

Choosing Your Yarn + Notions

A variety of yarn is used in the patterns in this book to provide a wide range in price, fiber content and weight. While thicker yarns may be more desirable to new crocheters due to the quick gratification, the same few crochet fundamentals are used in each pattern, regardless of whether the design calls for fingering weight or bulky weight. Throughout this book, the yarn weight does not correlate with the difficulty level of the pattern.

Substituting Yarn

Not every yarn used in this book may be accessible to you. To find a suitable yarn substitution for any yarn, visit www.yarnsub.com and type in the name of the yarn you are trying to match. This is an incredible resource for knitters and crocheters, filled with information comparing yardage, gauge, fiber content, price and so many more details you may want to consider when choosing your fiber.

You don't need to spend hundreds of dollars on yarn to yield a beautiful sweater. While luxurious fibers and hand-dyed yarns are a treat to work with, inexpensive department store brands can often achieve a similar result without breaking the bank. This book contains mostly budget-friendly yarns with a few higher-priced yarns mixed in. For every pattern that uses a more costly yarn, I've listed some budget-friendly alternatives with a lower price point that may be more accessible.

To keep the integrity of the fabric in any given pattern, you may want to use a similar fiber content, though this is by no means necessary. All you need to know is how your fiber behaves before choosing to use it in a design. For example, cotton yarns are usually quite heavy, and will drape differently than a 100% wool fiber. If replacing wool with cotton, you will probably want to shorten the length of your sweater and sleeves to account for the growth that will occur from using a heavier fiber. This is not to dissuade you from experimenting with your fiber choices—just be aware of how your chosen fiber behaves and adjust if necessary.

Check the Dye Lot

When working on large-scale projects that use a lot of yarn, as garments do, be sure to check the dye lots on your yarn before starting. Despite being labeled as the same color, skeins can appear drastically different if they come from different dye lots, an effect even more apparent once the garment is crocheted into fabric. Make sure the dye lot is the same for each skein before beginning.

Locking Stitch Markers Are Key

Locking stitch markers are used in every pattern in this book as a method of marking stitch placement, holding two layers of fabric together or securing panels in place to prepare for seaming. If you don't have any, you can use scrap yarn, bobby pins or anything else that you can clip or tie onto a stitch to serve the same purpose. While you can certainly complete these patterns without locking stitch markers, there are many useful applications for them, and I highly recommend an inexpensive set to use for your upcoming crochet projects. Get a lot, as these seem to always go missing!

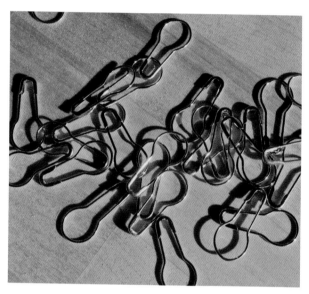

Understanding Gauge Swatches

Gauge swatches, also called tension swatches, are a crucial step in achieving a properly fitting sweater. Swatches are necessary for every pattern in this book, so whatever you do, don't skip this step. Many of these patterns consist solely of single crochet, double crochet or half double crochet rows, which makes swatching for most patterns quite straightforward; all you have to do is crochet a square using the specified stitch.

A few of the designs involve stitch patterns with two or more stitches: For example, a combination of single crochet and chain stitches to produce the granite stitch. On patterns using a mix of stitches, I've included specific gauge swatch instructions for each of these so you can be confident in your swatch.

If you plan to block your finished sweater, block your swatch before measuring gauge.

Always work a gauge swatch that is slightly larger than the measurements indicated. For example, if a gauge swatch is provided as follows:

4 x 4" (10 x 10 cm) = 16 stitches and 14 rows in single crochet

This means that a 4-inch (10-cm) square should consist of sixteen stitches across and fourteen rows in height. To get an accurate measurement, your sample must be slightly larger than a 4-inch (10-cm) square because you don't want any edge stitches to be included. Edge stitches will measure slightly different than the inner stitches, which are the ones that comprise your entire sweater. Remember: The whole point of swatching is to attempt to reproduce the stitches that will end up in your final sweater.

If Your Gauge Is Off, Here's What Will Happen . . .

Because this gauge measurement of stitches per 4 inches (10 cm) is repeated multiple times across the circumference of your sweater, a gauge swatch off by one or two stitches makes a significant difference.

For example, let's pretend that the total number of stitches in the bust for your size is 160, intended to create a garment with a 40-inch (102-cm) finished bust. If the pattern gauge is listed at sixteen stitches for every 4 inches (10 cm) but your gauge swatch has only 14 stitches for every 4 inches (10 cm), you will actually create a sweater with a finished bust that measures 45.7 inches (116 cm) instead of the intended 40 inches (102 cm)—almost two sizes larger than intended. An inaccuracy of two stitches in your gauge swatch may seem insignificant, but this can be the difference between a perfectly fitting sweater and one that is multiple sizes too big (or uncomfortably tight and unwearable) when multiplied across the circumference of your garment.

Because tension differs, two people can make the same pattern using the same hook and yarn and create two vastly different sized sweaters. Take the time to crochet a test swatch to make sure you are using the appropriate hook size for your unique tension, and you'll save yourself hours, or even days, of work and prevent having to rip back to rework the garment using a different hook size.

When choosing a hook, start off using the recommended hook size. Because all hooks differ, and the tension differs from person to person, you may need a different hook from the one that I used. If your gauge swatch has more stitches per 4 inches (10 cm), try swatching again with a larger hook size. If your gauge swatch has fewer stitches per 4 inches (10 cm), try swatching again with a smaller hook size.

Closet Staples

Everyday Wardrobe Essentials

There are a few patterns in this book that really jump out as definite wardrobe essentials. These are basic pieces that can be worn with a vast array of outfits and are suitable for almost any occasion. The designs in this chapter are intended to get the most wear because they are simple, refined and timeless. Each design is intended to blend seamlessly with your existing wardrobe—something you'll reach for time and time again and that won't go out of style. If you're like me, you're probably going to want one of these designs in every color.

Tastefully understated and capsule-wardrobe-approved, each piece within this chapter comes with endless mix-and-match potential.

Sacred Woods
Side-Split Sweater

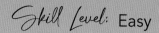

Skill Level: Easy

Meet Sacred Woods, a moody pullover sweater featuring vertical stitching, a relaxed fit and elegant side slits. Vertical rows are used to mimic tall, slender trees found in a forest, encouraging the sweater to lie gracefully on your body. This sweater is worked in simple stitches with minimal shaping, meaning you'll only need to refer to the pattern a couple times—perfect for distracted crocheting.

Long enough to wear with leggings, Sacred Woods is the ultimate grab-and-go piece. The dramatic side slits add dimension and movement while allowing more space in the hips for a great fit on both slim and curvy body types.

Construction

The body of this sweater is worked sideways as a long rectangle with a head opening in the center. After the body is folded in half at the shoulders and the sides are seamed, the sleeves are worked directly onto the body in joined rounds for minimal seaming. There is no visible seam separating the sleeves from the body, creating a smooth, visually pleasing continuity in the fabric; maintaining the same sideways back-and-forth rows creates the look of one seamless piece of fabric from wrist to wrist.

Materials

Yarn:
Worsted—Lion Brand Wool-Ease Yarn in Umber (80% acrylic, 20% wool)
197 yds (180 m) per 3-oz (85-g) ball
Find this yarn on lionbrand.com or visit yarnsub.com to find comparable substitutes.

ABBREVIATIONS
Written in U.S. crochet terms
ch: chain
dc: double crochet
dc2tog: double crochet 2 stitches together
FDC: foundation double crochet (see Foundation Stitches in the Techniques section on page 176)
rep: repeat
rnd(s): round(s)
sc: single crochet
scBLO: single crochet in the back loop only
sk: skip
sl st: slip stitch
st(s): stitch(es)
tch: turning chain

Yardage:
6 (7, 7, 8, 8) (8, 8, 9, 9) skeins or 1130 (1215, 1300, 1375, 1450) (1500, 1550, 1615, 1650) yds [1033 (1111, 1189, 1257, 1326) (1372, 1417, 1477, 1509) m]

Note: Budget friendly!
Substitute Lion Brand Wool-Ease Yarn with any similar worsted weight, category #4 yarn that matches gauge. Most fibers should produce a beautiful sweater.

Hook:
Size U.S. I/9 (5.5 mm) or size needed to obtain gauge

Notions:
Tapestry needle, locking stitch markers

(continued)

Gauge:
4 x 4" (10 x 10 cm) = 11.5 sts and 7.5 rows in double crochet

For Swatch:
Ch 18.

Row 1: Dc in 3rd st from hook and in each st across, turn. [16 dc]

Row 2–15: Ch 2, dc in each st across, turn.

Block your swatch. Measure the inner 4 inches (10 cm) of your blocked swatch to get the most accurate measurement.

Note on half stitches: When measuring your swatch, 4 inches (10 cm) should equal approximately 11.5 stitches and 7.5 rows.

Sacred Woods Sizing Chart

	A FINISHED BUST CIRCUMFERENCE	BUILT-IN POSITIVE EASE	B TOTAL LENGTH MEASURED FROM TOPS OF SHOULDERS	C SLEEVE LENGTH MEASURED FROM UNDERARM	D UPPER ARM CIRCUMFERENCE	E WRIST CIRCUMFERENCE
XS	39" 99 cm	9–11" 23–28 cm	29.5" 75 cm	17.5" 44 cm	14" 35 cm	9.25" 23 cm
S	44" 112 cm	10–12" 25–30 cm	29.5" 75 cm	16.5" 42 cm	14.5" 37 cm	9.75" 25 cm
M	48" 122 cm	10–12" 25–30 cm	29.5" 75 cm	15.5" 39 cm	15.25" 39 cm	9.75" 25 cm
L	52" 132 cm	10–12" 25–30 cm	29.5" 75 cm	14.5" 37 cm	16.75" 42 cm	9.75" 25 cm
XL	57" 145 cm	11–13" 28–33 cm	29.5" 75 cm	13.5" 34 cm	17.25" 44 cm	9.75" 25 cm
2X	59" 150 cm	9–11" 23–28 cm	29.5" 75 cm	13" 33 cm	19.5" 49 cm	10.25" 26 cm
3X	61" 155 cm	7–9" 18–23 cm	29.5" 75 cm	12" 30 cm	21" 53 cm	10.25" 26 cm
4X	63" 160 cm	5–7" 13–18 cm	29.5" 75 cm	11.5" 29 cm	21.5" 55 cm	11.5" 29 cm
5X	65" 165 cm	3–5" 8–13 cm	29.5" 75 cm	11" 28 cm	21.5" 55 cm	11.5" 29 cm

This chart shows the finished garment measurements. This sweater is designed to be worn with up to 13 inches (33 cm) of positive ease, depending on the size you are making. Find the finished bust measurement in this chart and refer to the built-in ease when choosing a size to make. For reference, the model is 5 feet, 4 inches (163 cm) tall with a 34-inch (86-cm) bust and is wearing a size small with a finished garment bust measurement of 44 inches (112 cm) with 10 inches (25 cm) of positive ease. If between sizes, size down.

For more information and tester photos, visit knitsnknots.ca/sacred-woods.

Sacred Woods Pattern

Schematic

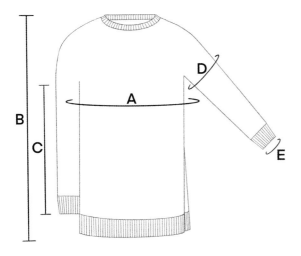

Body

A Note Before Beginning: The body of this sweater is worked in one piece. First, you will work a long rectangle, denoted as first side, then you will work a few shorter rows to create the back of the sweater. Next, you will work a similar section of shorter rows to become the front of the sweater. Last, you will work a joining row across the front and back sections to connect them, and then you will create the second side, identical to the first side. Once completed, the work is folded in half at the red line shown in the image below.

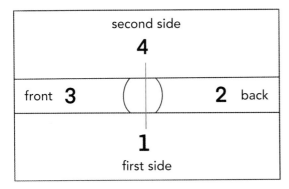

Figure 1: This diagram shows the order in which you will work the body of this sweater.

Customization Tip: For a longer or shorter sweater, add or subtract stitches in multiples of two; one stitch assigned to the front and one to the back.

For example, if you subtract a total of 20 stitches from your foundation row, 10 stitches will be eliminated from the front of your sweater and 10 stitches will be eliminated from the back of your sweater. So, when you work Section 2 and Section 3 (the Back and the Front), you will subtract 10 stitches from each of these counts and follow the rest of the pattern as written.

1. First Side

Row 1: FDC 150.

Rows 2–14 (16, 18, 20, 22) (22, 23, 24, 25): Ch 2, dc in each st across, turn. [150 dc]

2. Back

Next Row: Ch 2, dc in next 68 sts, dc2tog, turn. [69 dc]

Next 7 (7, 7, 7, 7) (9, 9, 9, 9) rows: Ch 2, dc in each st across, turn.

Stop here. Pull this loop up slightly or put a locking stitch marker around the live loop to hold it in place; you will come back to this after you work the front.

3. Front

With the Back section on your right, count 15 sts from back section (these 15 sts will remain unworked) and join new yarn with a sl st into the next (the 16th) st to begin working from the center toward the unworked edge, leaving a gap between the front and back, which will become the head opening.

Work first dc into the st after the sl st.

Next Row: Ch 2, dc in next st and in each st across, turn. [64 dc]

Next 7 (7, 7, 7, 7) (9, 9, 9, 9) rows: Ch 2, dc in each st across, turn.

Fasten off.

4. Second Side

Return to where you left off on the back panel and insert your hook into the live st to continue working with this yarn. Next, you will work across the Back section, create a chain, then work across the front section to connect this row so that you can work the second side to be identical to the first side.

Joining Row: Ch 2, dc in next 68 sts, 2 dc in next st, ch 15, 2 dc in first st of front panel, dc in each st across, turn. [135 dc; 15 ch]

Next 14 (16, 18, 20, 22) (22, 23, 24, 25) rows: Ch 2, dc in each st across, turn. [150 dc]

Do not fasten off, continue with the working yarn to complete the Bottom Ribbing.

Count 56 (55, 54, 52, 51) (48, 46, 45, 45) sts from all four corners and place a marker or scrap yarn in this st to help with sleeve placement later. You will come back to this.

Bottom Ribbing

Turn your work to begin working across the ends of the rows you just completed.

Set-Up Row: Ch 1, work 74 (82, 90, 98, 106) (110, 114, 118, 122) sc across the bottom edge by crocheting 2 sc for every row of dc as evenly as you can.

Ch 16.

Row 1: Sc in 2nd ch from hook and in each ch across, sl st in next 2 sts from Set-Up Row, turn. [15 sc]

Row 2: [No tch] Sk the 2 sl st you just made, scBLO in next 14 sts, sc in last st, turn.

Row 3: Ch 1, sc in first st, scBLO in next 14 sts, sl st in next 2 sts from Set-Up Row, turn.

Rep Rows 2–3 until you have worked your way across the entire Set-Up Row. Fasten off and weave in ends.

Attach yarn to one of the opposite unworked corners with a sl st and rep all Bottom Ribbing instructions.

Blocking

Block your work before proceeding. You can block your sweater at the end, but it is easiest to block the bottom ribbing of this sweater at this point, before it is seamed.

Block to a width of approximately 19.5 (22, 24, 26, 28.5) (29.5, 30.5, 31.5, 32.5)" (50 [56, 61, 66, 72] [75, 77, 80, 83] cm) and a length of 59 inches (150 cm).

Assembly

Fold your sweater in half at the shoulders so the bottom ribbing and your markers all line up (see the red fold-line in Figure 1). Starting from the bottom, line up the sides stitch-for-stitch. Use locking stitch markers to help with this if desired. Using a separate length of yarn and a tapestry needle, begin seaming at approximately 14 inches (36 cm) from the bottom to leave a side split.

For more (or less) of a split, begin seaming higher (or lower) than instructed.

Continue seaming up the sides using the whip stitch (see Techniques on page 167) or seaming method of your choice, but stop at the stitch right before the markers. The markers denote the first and last sleeve stitch. Fasten off, but do not weave in ends yet. After you have completed the first sleeve round, you can return to the side seam you stitched earlier to close any remaining gaps at the underarm.

Sleeves

You should now have your body assembled with armholes on either side. You should still have four stitch markers at the underarm (two per side) denoting the first and last sleeve stitch to help work the first round.

Attach new yarn at one of the markers with a sl st. (Make sure you are working in the direction necessary to keep the back-and-forth rows consistent.)

Round 1: Ch 2, dc in same st as sl st, dc in each st around to second marker, dc in second marked st, sl st into first dc to join rnd, turn. [40 (42, 44, 48, 50) (56, 60, 62, 62) dc]

> *Note:* The sleeves are worked in joined rnds; after each rnd, you will sl st into the first st to join the rnd and then turn your work to begin crocheting in the opposite direction.

Round 2: Ch 2, dc in each dc around, sl st to join, turn.

For the remainder of the sleeve, work the rnds as specified for your size below:

When instructed to decrease, work the rnd as follows: Ch 2, dc in first st, dc2tog, dc until 3 sts remain unworked, dc2tog, dc in last st, sl st to join, turn. [Decreases rnd by 2 sts]

Work every rnd that is not a decrease rnd as a Round 2 rep.

> *Notes:* Total rnds provided includes the first two rnds you have already completed.
>
> For longer or shorter sleeve than written for your size, simply add or subtract non-increase rnds as you see fit. Work your sleeve until it measures 2 inches (5 cm) shorter than your desired length.

Size XS: Work a total of 29 sleeve rnds, decreasing in the following rds: 20, 24, 28. [34 dc]

Size S: Work a total of 27 sleeve rnds, decreasing in the following rnds: 18, 22, 26. [36 dc]

Size M: Work a total of 26 sleeve rnds, decreasing in the following rnds: 14, 18, 22, 26. [36 dc]

Size L: Work a total of 24 sleeve rnds, decreasing in the following rnds: 4, 8, 12, 16, 20, 24. [36 dc]

Size XL: Work a total of 22 sleeve rnds, decreasing in the following rnds: 3, 6, 9, 12, 15, 18, 21. [36 dc]

Size 2X: Work a total of 21 sleeve rnds, decreasing in the following rnds: 4, 6, 8, 10, 12, 14, 16, 18, 20. [38 dc]

Size 3X: Work a total of 19 sleeve rnds, decreasing in the following rnds: 3, 5, 7, 9, 11, 13, 15–19. [38 dc]

Size 4X: Work a total of 18 sleeve rnds, decreasing in the following rnds: 3, 5, 7, 9, 11, 13, 15–18. [42 dc]

Size 5X: Work a total of 17 sleeve rnds, decreasing in the following rnds: 3, 5, 7, 9, 11, 13–17. [42 dc]

Rep Rows 2–3 until you have worked your way across the entire sleeve rnd. Fasten off, seam first and last row together and weave in ends.

Rep all instructions for the second sleeve.

At this point, return to your side seams and use these ends to close any gaps at the underarm.

Neckline

Attach yarn to the neckline at the center-back with a sl st.

Set-Up Rnd: Ch 1, sc in each st around neckline, sl st into first sc to join rnd.

> *Tip:* Work 1 sc into each regular st while working 2 sc for every dc row-end. The exact number of sts you end up with here is not important.

Neckline Ribbing

Ch 5.

Row 1: Sc in 2nd ch from hook and in each ch across, sl st into next 2 sts from Set-Up Rnd, turn. [4 sc]

Row 2: [No tch] Sk the 2 sl st you just made, scBLO in next 3 sts, sc in last st, turn.

Row 3: Ch 1, sc in first st, scBLO in next 3 sts, sl st into next 2 sts from Set-Up Rnd, turn.

Rep Rows 2–3 until you have worked your way across the entire Set-Up Rnd. Fasten off, seam first and last row together with a tapestry needle using the whip stitch or seaming method of your choice.

Weave in any remaining ends, and block your sweater to the dimensions listed in the Sizing Chart (page 18).

Sleeve Cuffs

Ch 10.

Row 1: Sc in 2nd ch from hook and in each ch across, sl st in next 2 sts from last sleeve rnd, turn. [9 sc]

Row 2: [No tch] Sk the 2 sl st you just made, scBLO in next 8 sts, sc in last st, turn.

Row 3: Ch 1, sc in first st, scBLO in next 8 sts, sl st in next 2 sts from last sleeve rnd, turn.

Lakeside Mist
Cardigan

The perfect everyday cardigan is as integral to your wardrobe as a classic white tee or a well-fitting pair of jeans. This charming, flowy cardigan is possibly the most versatile design in the entire book, a casual piece you'll be reaching for time and time again. The slim-fit sleeves perfectly balance this relaxed cardigan, while the eye is drawn to the statement collar, a finishing detail that really brings this design to life. Slip it on for a comfortable yet polished look for a casual night out or a cozy weekend outfit. One thing's for sure: You're going to need one in every color.

Construction

The body of this cardigan is worked in two identical pieces that get partially seamed together. The body is worked side-to-side, and the sleeves are worked bottom-up in joined rounds before being seamed onto the body.

Materials

Yarn:
Light Worsted—Berroco Ultra Alpaca in Stone Washed Mix (50% superfine alpaca, 50% Peruvian wool)

219 yds (200 m) per 3.5-oz (100-g) hank

Find this yarn on lovecrafts.com or visit yarnsub.com to find comparable substitutes.

Yardage:
9 (9, 10, 10, 10) (11, 11, 11, 12) hanks or 1775 (1825, 1975, 2025, 2175) (2200, 2250, 2350, 2425) yds [1624 (1669, 1806, 1852, 1989) (2012, 2058, 2149, 2218) m]

Note: Budget-friendly alternatives include Paintbox Yarns 100% Wool Worsted Superwash, Patons Classic Wool Worsted, Comfy Worsted (non-animal-fiber option), WeCrochet Simply Alpaca, Drops Lima Mix, Drops Puna.

ABBREVIATIONS
Written in U.S. crochet terms
ch: chain
ch-sp(s): chain space(s)
FSC: foundation single crochet (see Foundation Stitches in the Techniques section on page 172)
rep: repeat
rnd(s): round(s)
sc: single crochet
scBLO: single crochet in the back loop only
sk: skip
sl st: slip stitch
st(s): stitch(es)
tch: turning chain

Substitute Berroco Ultra Alpaca with any similar DK (category #3) or light worsted (category #4) yarn that matches gauge. This yarn is labeled as worsted, but feels thinner than most other worsted weight yarns.

Hook:
Size U.S. H/8 (5 mm) or size needed to obtain gauge

Notions:
Tapestry needle, several locking stitch markers

Gauge:
4 x 4" (10 x 10 cm) = 18.5 sts and 18 rows in stitch pattern, where each sc counts as a stitch and each ch counts as a stitch (see instructions below)

Ch 22.

Row 1: Sc in 2nd ch from hook, *ch 1, sk next ch, sc in next ch; rep from * to end of row, turn. [11 sc; 10 ch-sps]

Row 2: Ch 1, sc in first sc, *ch 1, sk next ch-sp, sc in next sc; rep from * to end of row, turn.

Rep Row 2 until you have at least 20 rows worked.

Block your swatch. Measure the inner 4 inches (10 cm) of your swatch to get the most accurate measurement.

Lakeside Mist Sizing Chart

	A FINISHED BUST CIRCUMFERENCE	B BUILT-IN POSITIVE EASE	C TOTAL LENGTH MEASURED FROM TOPS OF SHOULDERS TO BOTTOM OF CARDIGAN	D SLEEVE LENGTH MEASURED FROM UNDERARM	E UPPER ARM CIRCUMFERENCE	F WRIST CIRCUMFERENCE
XS	42" 107 cm	12–14" 30–36 cm	29" 74 cm	17" 43 cm	12" 30 cm	7.5" 19 cm
S	46" 117 cm	12–14" 30–36 cm	29" 74 cm	16" 41 cm	12.75" 32 cm	7.5" 19 cm
M	50" 127 cm	12–14" 30–36 cm	29" 74 cm	15" 38 cm	13" 33 cm	8" 20 cm
L	52" 132 cm	10–12" 25–30 cm	29" 74 cm	14.5" 37 cm	14" 36 cm	8" 20 cm
XL	54" 137 cm	8–10" 20–25 cm	29" 74 cm	13.75" 35 cm	15.75" 40 cm	8" 20 cm
2X	58" 147 cm	8–10" 20-25 cm	29" 74 cm	13" 33 cm	18" 46 cm	8.5" 22 cm
3X	60" 152 cm	6–8" 15–20 cm	29" 74 cm	12.5" 32 cm	18.75" 48 cm	8.5" 22 cm
4X	62" 157 cm	4–6" 10–15 cm	29" 74 cm	12" 30 cm	20" 51 cm	9" 23 cm
5X	66" 168 cm	4–6" 10–15 cm	29" 74 cm	11" 28 cm	20" 51 cm	9" 23 cm

This chart shows the finished garment measurements. This cardigan is designed to be worn with up to 14 inches (36 cm) of positive ease, depending on the size you are making. Find the finished bust measurement in this chart and refer to the built-in ease when choosing a size to make. For reference, the model is 5 feet, 4 inches (163 cm) tall with a 34-inch (86-cm) bust and is wearing a size small with a finished garment bust measurement of 46 inches (117 cm) worn with 12 inches (30 cm) of positive ease. If between sizes, size down.

For more information and tester photos, visit knitsnknots.ca/lakeside-mist.

Lakeside Mist Pattern

Schematic

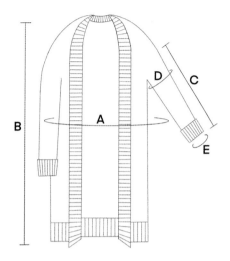

Body Panel (Make 2)

> *Note:* The beginning foundation chain is what determines the length of your cardigan. This chain is the length of the back and front combined. To adjust the length, add or subtract from this foundation chain in multiples of 4. Make note of how many multiples of 4 you adjusted.

Row 1: FSC 271, place marker in 20th st from each end to help you remember where the ribbing will be placed. (After working into a marked st, move the marker up to the new st each row.)

Row 2: Ch 1 (does not count as a st here and throughout), sc in first st, scBLO in next 19 sts, sc in next st, *ch 1, sk next st, sc in next st; rep from * across row until 20 sts remain unworked, scBLO in next 19 sts, sc in last st, turn. [20 sts of ribbing at each end, 116 sc; 115 ch-sps in the middle]

Row 3: Ch 1, sc in first st, scBLO in next 19 sts, sc in next sc, *ch 1, sk next ch-sp, sc in next sc; rep from * across row until 20 sts remain unworked, scBLO in next 19 sts, sc in last st, turn.

Rep Row 3 until work measures 7 (8, 9, 9.5, 10) (11, 11.5, 12, 13)" (18 [20, 23, 24, 25] [28, 29, 30, 33] cm). Do not fasten off, continue with working yarn to create the Back-Neck.

Back-Neck

You are going to work a few rows here that will become the back of your sweater.

> *Note:* If you adjusted the length of your cardigan, for every multiple of 4 stitches you adjusted to the foundation chain, add or subtract 1 repeat to the number provided in Row 1. For example, if you add 8 stitches to your foundation chain (two multiples of four stitches), you will work 2 additional repeats in Row 1 and repeat the sequence 56 times instead of 54 times.

Row 1: Ch 1, sc in first st, scBLO in next 19 sts, sc in next sc, *ch 1, sk next ch-sp, sc in next sc; rep from * 54 more times. [20 sts of ribbing; 56 sc and 55 ch-sps after ribbing]

Row 2: Ch 1, sc in first sc, *ch 1, sk next ch-sp, sc in next sc; rep from * until 20 sts remain unworked, scBLO in next 19 sts, sc in last st, turn.

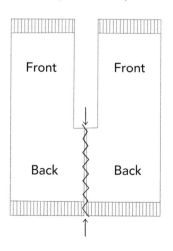

Rep Rows 1–2 until your entire panel measures 9 (10, 11, 11.5, 12) (13, 13.5, 14, 15)" (23 [25, 28, 29, 30] [33, 34, 36, 38] cm) from foundation row along this back-neck section.

Fasten off, leaving a long tail for seaming.

Lay your body panels next to each other with the back-neck (the blue zig-zag line in the facing diagram) sections touching as shown in the illustration. Use your long tails to seam the panels together along the back-neck with a tapestry needle using the whip stitch (see Techniques on page 167) or seaming method of your choice.

Fold the front panels down over the back panels. Starting from the bottom, seam the sides using the whip stitch or seaming method of your choice. Stop at approximately 6.5 (7, 7, 7, 8) (9, 10, 10, 10)" (16 [18, 18, 18, 20] [23, 26, 26, 26] cm) from the tops of the shoulders to leave space to attach the sleeves. You will come back to this side seam when you sew on the sleeves to close up any remaining gaps.

Sleeves (Make 2)

Cuff

Ch 21, leaving a tail for seaming the cuff.

Row 1: Sc in 2nd ch from hook and in each ch across, turn. [20 sc]

Row 2: Ch 1, sc in first sc, scBLO in each st across until 1 st remains, sc in last st, turn.

Rep Row 2 until you have a total of 35 (35, 37, 37, 37) (39, 39, 41, 41) rows.

Turn your work to begin working across the ends of the rows you just completed. Treat each row-end as a stitch.

Rnd 1: Ch 1, sc into first row-end, *ch 1, sk next row-end, sc in next row-end; rep from * to end of row, sl st into first sc to join rnd, turn. [18 (18, 19, 19, 19) (20, 20, 21, 21) sc; 17 (17, 18, 18, 18) (19, 19, 20, 20) ch-sp]

With a tapestry needle, seam your cuff closed with the tail from your beginning ch using the whip stitch or seaming method of your choice.

For the remainder of the sleeve, work the rnds as specified for your size below:

When instructed to increase, work the rnd as follows: Ch 1, sc in first sc, ch 1, sc in first ch-sp, ch 1, sc in next sc, *ch 1, sk next ch-sp, sc in next sc; rep from * until 1 sc remains, ch 1, sc in next ch-sp, ch 1, sc in last sc, sl st into first sc to join, turn. [Increases rnd by 2 sc and 2 ch]

Every rnd that is not an increase rnd is worked as follows: Ch 1, sc in first sc, *ch 1, sk next ch-sp, sc in next sc; rep from * to end of rnd, sl st into first sc to join, turn.

Note: Total rnds provided includes the first rnd you have already completed.

XS: Work a total of 76 rnds, while increasing in the following rnds: 2, 10, 18, 26, 34. [28 sc; 27 ch-sp]

S (M): Work a total of 72 (67) rnds, while increasing in the following rnds: 2, 10, 18, 26, 34, 42. [30 (31) sc; 29 (30) ch-sp]

L: Work a total of 65 rnds, while increasing in the following rnds: 2, 8, 14, 20, 26, 32, 38. [33 sc; 32 ch-sp]

XL: Work a total of 62 rnds, while increasing in the following rnds: 2, 8, 14, 20, 26, 32, 38, 44, 50. [37 sc; 36 ch-sp]

2X: Work a total of 58 rnds, while increasing in the following rnds: 2, 7, 12, 17, 22, 27, 32, 37, 42, 47, 52. [42 sc; 41 ch-sp]

3X: Work a total of 56 rnds, while increasing in the following rnds: 2, 6, 10, 14, 18, 22, 26, 30, 34, 38, 42, 46. [44 sc; 43 ch-sp]

4X (5X): Work a total of 54 (49) rnds, while increasing in the following rnds: 2, 5, 9, 12, 16, 19, 23, 26, 30, 33, 37, 40, 44. [47 (47) sc; 46 (46) ch-sp]

Fasten off, leaving a 24-inch (61-cm) tail for attaching the sleeve to the body panels.

Collar

Attach yarn to one of the bottom inside corners with a sl st to begin the collar.

Set-Up Row: Ch 1, sc evenly around the entire collar, up around the neckline and back down the opposite side, working into each sc and each ch-sp. Once you reach the opposite bottom corner, turn work to begin working back on this Set-Up Row.

Ribbing

Ch 21.

Row 1: Sc in 2nd ch from hook and in each ch across, sl st into next 2 sts from Set-Up Row to join row to body, turn. [20 sc]

Row 2: [No tch] Sk 2 sl sts just worked, scBLO in each st until 1 st remains, sc in last st, turn. [19 scBLO; 1 sc]

Row 3: [No tch] Sc in first st, scBLO in each st to end of row, sl st into next 2 sts from Set-Up Row, turn.

Rep Rows 2–3 until you have worked your way around the entire collar and reached the opposite bottom corner.

Fasten off, weave in any remaining ends and block your sweater to the dimensions listed in the Sizing Chart (page 25).

Assembly

Lay your work flat. Place the sleeves at the arm openings with the seam pointing down toward the armpit. Use locking stitch markers to help align the sts evenly around the sleeve openings on the body panels. With a tapestry needle, use the tail end to seam the sleeve in place using the whip stitch or any seaming method of your choice. When seaming your sleeves onto your sweater, make sure to keep this seam loose and do not pull tight in order to maintain some stretch, otherwise this seam will pucker and restrict your arms during wear. Use the tail from the side seam to close any remaining gaps. Weave in ends.

Distant Fog
Sweater Dress

Equal parts casual and graceful, Distant Fog is an infinitely versatile piece that doesn't just enhance an outfit but *becomes* the outfit. This simple design paired with a relaxed fit makes Distant Fog a staple piece that can be worn on any occasion without feeling overdressed. Soft elements like the deep, curving neckline and the delicate split hem help bring a lightness to this boxy dress. Changing the length is a great way to breathe new life into a design without needing to modify any pattern math, and this humble sweater has the potential to be worn as a hip-length sweater or a dress that lands at the thigh for a comfortable, approachable outfit that suits your personal taste. Try defining your waistline with a belt for a more tailored fit.

The yarn choice can lead this design in many interesting directions. Hold a DK yarn together with mohair for a fuzzy halo effect or choose a fiber with a drape you would love to wear. Distant Fog is a sweater version of the Mountain Peaks Cardigan (page 137). Both designs are comprised of the same stitch, with angled shaping around the neckline, demonstrating how the slightest change in detail can create an entirely fresh design.

Construction

This sweater is worked in four panels: a front panel, a back panel and two sleeves. The front and back body panels are worked first and seamed together along the shoulders and the sides, leaving openings for the sleeves to be attached. The sleeves are worked next, from the wrist upward in joined, turned rounds.

Materials

Yarn:
Aran—WeCrochet Simply Alpaca Aran in Alfie (100% superfine alpaca)
246 yds (225 m) per 3.5-oz (100-g) hank
Find this yarn on crochet.com or visit yarnsub.com to find comparable substitutes.

Yardage:
7 (8, 8, 8, 8) (9, 9, 10, 10) hanks or 1650 (1725, 1850, 1900, 1975) (2075, 2225, 2325, 2425) yds [1509 (1578, 1692, 1738, 1806) (1897, 2034, 2126, 2217) m]

Note on Yardage: The yardage listed here is for the length provided in the Sizing Chart on page 31. For a longer sweater, additional yardage will be required.

Note: Budget-friendly alternatives include WeCrochet Palette held double, Lion Brand Touch of Alpaca.

Substitute WeCrochet Simply Alpaca Aran with any similar worsted (category #4) or DK (category #3) weight yarn that matches gauge. This particular yarn is labeled as a heavy worsted/aran weight, but it feels thinner, much like a DK weight yarn. When choosing a yarn, choose a fiber that gives you the best drape, one that you would like to wear against your skin for long periods of time. Any fiber should work out fine.

To match the look of the fiber used in this sample, choose an alpaca yarn. If you are prone to itching, choose an alpaca yarn that specifies "baby alpaca" as this is the softest type, or choose a different fiber altogether. Simply Alpaca is plied with a soft haze; a similar look can be achieved by using any DK fiber of your choosing paired with a mohair or Suri alpaca yarn.

Hook:
Size U.S. G/7 (4.5 mm) or size needed to obtain gauge

Notions:
Tapestry needle, several locking stitch markers to help with seaming

Gauge:
5 x 5" (13 x 13 cm) = 22 sts and 17 rows in half double crochet

ABBREVIATIONS
Written in U.S. crochet terms
ch: chain
hdc: half double crochet
hdc2tog: half double crochet 2 stitches together
rep: repeat
rnd(s): round(s)
sc: single crochet
sl st: slip stitch
st(s): stitch(es)

Schematic

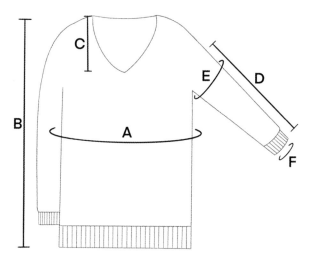

Distant Fog Sizing Chart

	A FINISHED BUST CIRCUMFERENCE	B TOTAL LENGTH MEASURED FROM TOPS OF SHOULDERS TO BOTTOM OF CARDIGAN	C V-NECK DEPTH MEASURED FROM TOPS OF SHOULDERS	D SLEEVE LENGTH MEASURED FROM UNDERARM	E UPPER ARM CIRCUMFERENCE	F WRIST CIRCUMFERENCE
XS	35.5" 90 cm	31" 79 cm	7.5" 19 cm	21.25" 54 cm	11.5" 29 cm	9" 23 cm
S	39.5" 100 cm	31" 79 cm	7.5" 19 cm	21" 53 cm	11.75" 30 cm	9.5" 24 cm
M	43.5" 110 cm	31" 79 cm	7.5" 19 cm	20" 51 cm	12.75" 32 cm	9.5" 24 cm
L	47.5" 121 cm	31" 79 cm	7.5" 19 cm	19" 48 cm	13.75" 35 cm	9.5" 24 cm
XL	52" 132 cm	31" 79 cm	7.5" 19 cm	18" 46 cm	15.25" 39 cm	10.25" 26 cm
2X	56" 142 cm	31" 79 cm	7.5" 19 cm	17" 43 cm	17" 43 cm	10.25" 26 cm
3X	60" 152 cm	31" 79 cm	7.5" 19 cm	16" 41 cm	18.75" 48 cm	10.25" 26 cm
4X	64" 163 cm	31" 79 cm	7.5" 19 cm	15.5" 39 cm	20" 51 cm	11" 28 cm
5X	68" 173 cm	31" 79 cm	7.5" 19 cm	14.5" 37 cm	20" 51 cm	11" 28 cm

This chart shows the finished garment measurements. This sweater is designed to be worn with approximately 5 to 8 inches (13 to 20 cm) of positive ease. When choosing a size, find the bust measurement in this chart that equals approximately 5 to 8 inches (13 to 20 cm) larger than your actual bust measurement and make this size. If this garment circumference (Column A) is smaller than the circumference of your hips, size up to accommodate your widest circumference measurement. For reference, the model is 5 feet, 4 inches (163 cm) tall with a 34-inch (86-cm) bust and is wearing a size small with a finished garment bust measurement of 39.5 inches (100 cm). If between sizes, size down.

For more information and tester photos, visit knitsnknots.ca/distant-fog.

Distant Fog Pattern

Front Panel

Bottom Hem
Ch 16 (16, 16, 16, 18) (18, 18, 20, 20).

Row 1: Hdc in 2nd ch from hook and in each ch across, turn. [15 (15, 15, 15, 17) (17, 17, 19, 19) hdc]

Row 2: Ch 1 (does not count as a st here and throughout), hdc in each hdc across, turn.

Rep Row 2 until you have worked a total of 52 (58, 64, 70, 76) (82, 88, 94, 100) rows.

Keep in mind that the width of this bottom hem should measure approximately 17.75 (19.75, 21.75, 23.75, 26) (28, 30, 32, 34)" (45 [50, 55, 60, 66] [71, 76, 81, 86] cm) once blocked.

Body
After the last row, turn your work to begin working into the edges of the rows you just completed.

Row 1: Ch 1, *work 3 hdc for every 2 rows of ribbing; rep from * all the way across your entire length of ribbing, turn. [78 (87, 96, 105, 114) (123, 132, 141, 150) hdc]

Row 2: Ch 1, hdc into each st to end of row, turn.

Rep last row until you have worked a total of 68 (68, 68, 68, 66) (66, 66, 66, 66) rows.

> *Customization Tip:* For a longer (or shorter) sweater, work additional (or fewer) rows than instructed above. Make note of how many rows you added or eliminated so that you can make the same alteration to your back panel.

V-Neck
Side 1

Row 1: Ch 1, hdc in next 35 (39, 44, 48, 53) (57, 62, 66, 70) sts, hdc2tog, hdc in next st, turn. [37 (41, 46, 50, 55) (59, 64, 68, 72) hdc]

Row 2: Ch 1, hdc in first st, [hdc2tog] 2 times, hdc in each st to end of row, turn. [35 (39, 44, 48, 53) (57, 62, 66, 70) hdc]

Row 3: Ch 1, hdc in each st to last 3 sts, hdc2tog, hdc in last st, turn. [34 (38, 43, 47, 52) (56, 61, 65, 69) hdc]

Row 4–9: Rep Rows 2 and 3. [25 (29, 34, 38, 43) (47, 52, 56, 60) hdc]

Row 10: Ch 1, hdc in each st to end of row, turn.

Row 11: Ch 1, hdc in each st to last 3 sts, hdc2tog, hdc in last st, turn. [24 (28, 33, 37, 42) (46, 51, 55, 59) hdc]

Row 12–15: Rep Rows 10 and 11. [22 (26, 31, 35, 40) (44, 49, 53, 57) hdc]

Row 16–25: Rep Row 10.

For a deeper (or more modest) neckline, rep last row (or decrease reps of last row) until desired depth.

Fasten off, leaving a 16-inch (41-cm) tail for seaming the shoulder.

Lay your work with the completed Side 1 on the right. You are going to work Side 2 onto the main body panel to mirror Side 1. Count 2 (3, 2, 3, 2) (3, 2, 3, 4) sts from completed Row 1 of Side 1 and insert your hook into the next st, leaving these sts unworked and creating a small gap between the two sides. Attach with a sl st.

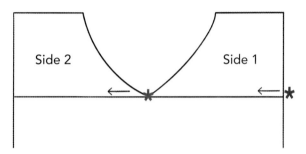

This diagram shows the direction in which you will be working to create Side 1 and Side 2. You will begin at each asterisk and work in the direction of the arrows.

Row 1: Ch 1, hdc in same st as sl st, hdc2tog, hdc in each st to end of row, turn. [37 (41, 46, 50, 55) (59, 64, 68, 72) hdc]

Row 2: Ch 1, hdc in each st to last 5 sts, [hdc2tog] 2 times, hdc in last st, turn. [35 (39, 44, 48, 53) (57, 62, 66, 70) hdc]

Row 3: Ch 1, hdc in first st, hdc2tog, hdc in each st to end of row, turn. [34 (38, 43, 47, 52) (56, 61, 65, 69) hdc]

Row 4–9: Rep Rows 2 and 3. [25 (29, 34, 38, 43) (47, 52, 56, 60) hdc]

Row 10: Ch 1, hdc in each st to end of row, turn.

Row 11: Ch 1, hdc in first st, hdc2tog, hdc in each st to end of row, turn. [24 (28, 33, 37, 42) (46, 51, 55, 59) hdc]

Row 12–15: Rep Rows 10 and 11. [22 (26, 31, 35, 40) (44, 49, 53, 57) hdc]

Row 16–25: Rep Row 10.

If you adjusted the V-neck depth on Side 1, make the same adjustment to Side 2.

Fasten off, leaving a 16-inch (41-cm) tail for seaming the shoulder. Block to the dimensions listed in the Sizing Chart (page 31).

Back Panel

Rep instructions from Front Panel up to and including Row 2 of the Body.

Rep last row until you have worked a total of 93 (93, 93, 93, 91) (91, 91, 91, 91) rows.

If you adjusted the length on the front panel, make the same adjustment on this back panel. Fasten off, weave in ends. Block to the dimensions listed in the Sizing Chart (page 31).

Partial Assembly

You are going to seam the shoulders and sides of your sweater before completing the sleeves. This way, you can try on your sweater and pin the sleeves in place as you work them to ensure the sleeves are the right length for your arms before cutting your yarn and seaming the entire sweater together.

Lay your blocked front panel over the top of your blocked back panel. There is no right side or wrong side. Use locking stitch markers to align your stitches.

When seaming the sides, begin just above the bottom ribbing in order to create a split hem. If you don't want a split hem, start at the very bottom. With a tapestry needle and a separate length of yarn measuring approximately 40 inches (102 cm), seam the sides of your sweater using the whip stitch (see Techniques on page 167) or seaming method of your choice, leaving at least 7 (7, 7, 8, 8) (10, 10, 11, 11)" (18 [18, 18, 20, 20] [25, 25, 28, 28] cm) from the tops of shoulders unseamed to create space for attaching the sleeves. You will come back to this seam, so don't fasten just yet. Rep for both sides.

Align the tops of the shoulders stitch-for-stitch on the front and back panels, using locking stitch markers to help ensure your stitches are properly aligned. With a tapestry needle, seam along the tops of the shoulders using the whip stitch or seaming method of your choice. Fasten off and weave in your ends. Rep for both shoulders.

Neckline Finishing

Decide which side you would like to wear as the right side and lay your work flat in front of you with the front panel right side facing you. Attach new yarn to the neckline at the left shoulder seam (the seam on your right) with a sl st to begin working down the neckline. Ch 1, sc evenly down the V-neck and back up until reaching the opposite shoulder seam. Sl st across the top of the back to reach the beginning point, sl st into first sc to join. Fasten off and weave in the ends.

Now that your front and back panels are seamed together, you are ready to start the sleeves.

Sleeves (Make 2)

Cuff

Ch 16, leaving a 12-inch (30-cm) tail for seaming the sleeve cuff closed.

Row 1: Hdc in 2nd ch from hook and in each ch across, turn. [15 hdc]

Row 2: Ch 1, hdc in each hdc to end of row, turn.

Rep Row 2 until you have a total of 26 (28, 28, 28, 30) (30, 30, 32, 32) rows completed.

After the last row, turn your work to begin working into the edges of the rows you just completed.

Row 1: Ch 1, *work 3 hdc for every 2 rows of ribbing; rep from * all the way across your entire cuff, connect your row by working a sl st into the first hdc to join in the round, turn. [39 (42, 42, 42, 45) (45, 45, 48, 48) hdc]

With a tapestry needle, use the tail from your ch to seam the first and last rows of ribbing together to form a tube using the whip stitch or seaming method of your choice.

The sleeves will be worked in joined rnds, turning your work after each rnd.

For the remainder of the sleeve, work the rnds as specified for your size below:

When instructed to increase, work the rnd as follows: Ch 1, hdc in first st, 2 hdc in next st, hdc around until 2 sts remain unworked, 2 hdc in next st, hdc in last st, sl st into first hdc to join, turn. [Increases rnd by 2 sts]

Every rnd that is NOT an increase rnd is worked as follows: Ch 1, hdc in each st around, sl st into first hdc to join, turn.

Follow your size only; total number of rnds given includes Rnd 1 you just completed.

Size XS: Work a total of 61 rnds, increasing in the following rnds: 10, 20, 30, 40, 50, 60. [51 hdc]

Size S: Work a total of 60 rnds, increasing in the following rnds: 12, 24, 36, 48, 60. [52 hdc]

Size 3X: Work a total of 43 rnds, increasing in the following rnds: 2, 4, 6, 8, 10, 12, 14, 16, 18, 20, 22, 24, 26, 28, 30, 32, 34, 37, 40. [83 hdc]

Size 4X: Work a total of 41 rnds, increasing in the following rnds: 2, 4, 6, 8, 10, 12, 14, 16, 18, 20, 22, 24, 26, 28, 30, 32, 34, 36, 38, 40. [88 hdc]

Size 5X: Work a total of 38 rnds, increasing in the following rnds: 3–6, 8, 10, 12, 14, 16, 18, 20, 22, 24, 26, 28, 30, 32, 34, 36, 38. [88 hdc]

Once satisfied with the sleeve length, fasten off, leaving a 24-inch (61-cm) tail for seaming the sleeve onto the body. Block your sleeves before seaming, if desired.

Assembly

Lay the sleeves in place with the seam at the bottom (toward the underarm). Use stitch markers to attach the sleeve onto the body. Make sure to stretch the sleeve over the body stitches enough to avoid a tight sleeve seam. You can stretch to approximately 3 sleeve stitches for every 2 rows of the body as a guideline. At this point, try your sweater on before cutting your yarn, and make any length adjustments if necessary.

With a tapestry needle and the tail you left after finishing the sleeve, loosely seam the sleeve to the body using the whip stitch or seaming method of your choice. Make sure to do this loosely and do not pull your yarn tight as you stitch, otherwise, the seam will feel tight and restricting. You want your seam to be loose so that your sleeve opening has some stretch, just like the rest of the sweater.

Return to the side seams you stitched earlier to close any remaining gaps at the underarm.

Weave in any remaining ends and block your sweater to the dimensions listed in the Sizing Chart (page 31).

Size M: Work a total of 56 rnds, increasing in the following rnds: 8, 16, 24, 32, 40, 48, 56. [56 hdc]

Size L: Work a total of 53 rnds, increasing in the following rnds: 5, 10, 15, 20, 25, 30, 35, 40, 45. [60 hdc]

Size XL: Work a total of 49 rnds, increasing in the following rnds: 4, 8, 12, 16, 20, 24, 28, 32, 36, 40, 44. [67 hdc]

Size 2X: Work a total of 46 rnds, increasing in the following rnds: 3, 6, 9, 12, 15, 18, 21, 24, 27, 30, 33, 36, 39, 42, 45. [75 hdc]

Infinite Prairies
Poncho

The prairies have a beauty that is subtle and understated, much like this design. Infinite Prairies is a structured yet graceful fall transitional piece designed for those brisk autumn days that demand a second layer. Serving the needs of both fashion and function, the turtleneck will keep you warm while bringing a polished element to this everyday piece. Slip your Infinite Prairies poncho over any outfit or try wearing a fitted, long-sleeve shirt underneath and pair with leggings and boots for a laid-back, comfortable outfit.

Made with bulky yarn and tall stitches, this quick project can easily be completed within just a few days. The playful columns of puff stitches add a fun element that will keep you engaged from start to finish.

Construction

This poncho has a circular yoke construction, worked from the top down. To make the Infinite Prairies poncho, you begin with the turtleneck, and then work the puff stitch pattern in joined rounds, increasing every few rounds until reaching the depth at which you will place the armholes. Next, two separate sections are worked to create space for the arms, and then re-joined to work in rounds until your desired length.

Materials

Yarn:
Bulky—Lion Brand Hue and Me in Desert (80% acrylic, 20% wool)

137 yds (125 m) per 4.4-oz (125-g) skein

Find this yarn on lionbrand.com or visit yarnsub.com to find comparable substitutes.

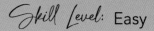
Skill Level: Easy

Yardage:
11 (12, 14, 15) skeins or 1450 (1600, 1800, 1950) yds [1326 (1464, 1646, 1784) m]

Note: Budget friendly!

Substitute Hue and Me for any similar bulky weight, category #5 yarn that matches gauge. Any fiber content should work out just fine. The only thing you may want to keep in mind is choosing a fiber that won't shed too much, because this is a piece that will be worn over another outfit.

Hook:
Size U.S. I/9 (5.5 mm) or size needed to obtain gauge

Notions:
Tapestry needle, three to four stitch markers

Main Gauge:
4 x 4" (10 x 10 cm) = 10 sts and 6 rows in double crochet

Turtleneck Gauge:
4 x 4" (10 x 10 cm) = 13 sts and 11 rows in single crochet in the back loops only (unstretched)

Make sure you check your gauge for the Turtleneck as well. Use whatever hook allows you to achieve the turtleneck gauge, or your desired fit for the turtleneck. You might match gauge with the same hook, or you might need to use a different hook to achieve the proper gauge for this ribbed turtleneck. This additional turtleneck gauge is included here to help you produce a final product with the best fit possible.

ABBREVIATIONS
Written in U.S. crochet terms
ch: chain
ch-sp: chain space
dc: double crochet
PM: place marker
Puff: [yarn over, insert hook into st, yarn over and pull up a loop] 5 times into designated stitch (11 loops on hook), yarn over and pull through all 11 loops on hook. (Note that when working the Puffs, you will find it helpful to pull your loops up a little bit to make it easier to pull through all the loops on your hook.)
rep: repeat
rnd(s): round(s)
sc: single crochet
scBLO: single crochet in the back loop only
sk: skip
sl st: slip stitch
st(s): stitch(es)

Schematic

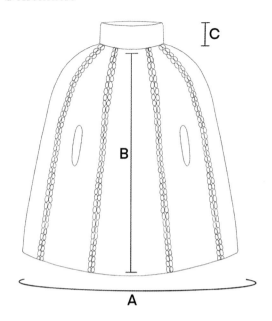

Infinite Prairies Sizing Chart

	A CIRCUMFERENCE MEASURED AT WIDEST POINT ALONG BOTTOM	BUILT-IN POSITIVE EASE	B TOTAL LENGTH NOT INCLUDING TURTLENECK	C TURTLENECK HEIGHT MEASURED UNFOLDED
XS	50" 127 cm	20–22" 51–56 cm	29" 74 cm	6.5" 17 cm
S/M/L	57" 145 cm	15–25" 38–64 cm	29" 74 cm	6.5" 17 cm
XL/2X/3X	63" 160 cm	9–19" 23–48 cm	29" 74 cm	6.5" 17 cm
4X/5X	70" 178 cm	8–14" 20–36 cm	29" 74 cm	6.5" 17 cm

This chart shows the finished garment measurements. The garment is designed to be oversized, worn with 8 to 25 inches (20 to 64 cm) of positive ease depending on the size you are making. Find the finished circumference measurement in this chart and refer to the built-in ease when choosing a size to make. For example, the model is 5 feet, 4 inches (163 cm) tall with a 34-inch (86-cm) bust and is wearing a size S/M/L with a finished garment circumference measurement of 57 inches (145 cm), worn with 23 inches (58 cm) of positive ease. If between sizes, size down.

For more information and tester photos, visit knitsnknots.ca/infinite-prairies.

Infinite Prairies Pattern

Turtleneck

Ch 21, leaving a 12-inch (30-cm) tail for seaming the turtleneck.

Customization Tip: For a shorter (or taller) turtleneck than the sample shown, work fewer (or additional) chains here as you see fit.

Row 1: Sc in 2nd ch from hook and in each ch across, turn. [20 sc]

Row 2: Ch 1, scBLO in each st across, turn. [20 scBLO]

Rep Row 2 until you have a total of 56 rows completed.

Turn your work to begin working across the ends of the rows you just completed.

Joining Rnd: Ch 1, work 1 sc into the ends of each row of ribbing, then bring your first and last st together to form a tube, sl st into first sc to join rnd, turn. [56 sc]

With a tapestry needle, seam your turtleneck closed using the whip stitch (see Techniques on page 167) or seaming method of your choice with the tail from your beginning ch.

Body

Rnd 1: Ch 2, dc in first 1 (2, 3, 3) sts, (Puff, ch 2, Puff) in next st, [dc in next 6 sts, (Puff, ch 2, Puff) in next st] 7 times, dc in last 5 (4, 3, 3) sts, sl st into first dc to join rnd, turn. [48 dc; 16 Puffs]

Rnd 2 (Increase Rnd): Ch 2, [dc in each dc until next Puff, dc in next Puff, (Puff, ch 2, Puff) into center ch2-sp from row below, dc in next Puff] 8 times, dc in each dc to end of rnd, sl st to join, turn. [64 dc; 16 Puffs]

Rnd 3: Ch 2, [dc in each dc until next Puff, sk Puff, (Puff, ch 2, Puff) into center ch2-sp from row below, sk next Puff] 8 times, dc in each dc to end of rnd, sl st to join, turn.

Rep Rnd 2 and 3 two (three, four, five) more times. [96 (112, 128, 144) dc; 16 Puffs]

At this point, you should have worked a total of 7 (9, 11, 13) rnds. You should have 12 (14, 16, 18) dc in between each Puff.

Work 7 (5, 4, 2) rnds as Rnd 3 reps.

At this point, you should have a total of 14 (14, 15, 15) rounds completed.

Split for Sleeve Opening
Section 1

To create sleeve openings without interrupting the stitch pattern, you will work two sections in back-and-forth rows, creating two armhole openings, and then connect them again to close up the armholes. For reference, you are working from the asterisk in Figure 1, then working back and forth on this section only (this section is denoted with a "1"). The blue line is the seam from joining rnds—where each of your rnds up to this point have started and finished.

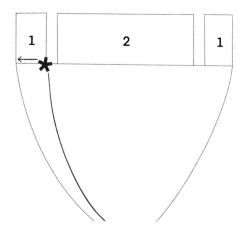

Figure 1

All Sizes

Row 15 (15, 16, 16): Ch 2, dc in each dc until first Puff, sk Puff, (Puff, ch 2, Puff) into center ch2-sp from row below, sk next Puff, [dc in each dc until next Puff, sk Puff, (Puff, ch 2, Puff) into center ch2-sp from row below, sk next Puff] 5 times, dc in next 4 (6, 8, 9) sts, stop here, leave next st unworked, PM in next st (you will return to this in Section 2), turn. [68 (82, 96, 108) dc; 12 Puffs]

Row 16 (16, 17, 17)–27: Ch 2, dc in each dc until first Puff, sk Puff, (Puff, ch 2, Puff) into center ch2-sp from row below, sk next Puff, [dc in each dc until next Puff, sk Puff, (Puff, ch 2, Puff) into center ch2-sp from row below, sk next Puff] 5 times, dc in each dc to end of row, turn.

Pull up this live loop and put a st marker in it to hold it in place. You will come back to it after completing Section 2. When you return to this live loop, you will continue working in the same direction as Row 27, working over Section 2.

Section 2

To create Section 2, lay your work out flat with the unworked section of Row 15 facing you. You are going to attach yarn into the marked st (the second available stitch from the right-hand side) as shown by the asterisk in Figure 2, leaving 1 st unworked after the first completed section.

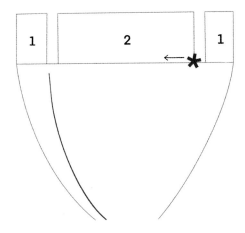

Figure 2

Row 15 (15, 16, 16): With new yarn, join yarn with a sl st 2 sts away from the first section, leaving 1 st unworked between Sections 1 and 2, ch 2, *dc in each st up to next Puff, sk Puff, (Puff, ch 2, Puff) into center ch2-sp from row below, sk next Puff; rep from * once more, dc in each st across, leaving 1 st unworked between Section 1 and Section 2, turn. [26 (28, 30, 34) dc; 4 Puffs]

Row 16 (16, 17, 17)–26: Ch 2, *dc in each st until first Puff, sk Puff, (Puff, ch 2, Puff) into center ch2-sp from row below, sk next Puff; rep from * once more, dc in each dc to end of row, turn.

Cut yarn.

Insert your hook into the st where you left off in Section 1.

At this point, you have worked Row 27 over Section 1, but have not yet worked Row 27 over Section 2. Now you are going to continue Row 27, working over Section 2.

Your work should now be connected, and you are set up to continue working in joined, turned rnds just as before splitting for the armholes.

Rnd 28: Rep Row 3; dc into each of the ch1-sps you worked in Row 27 to close the armholes, treating them as a dc.

Rnds 29–44: Rep Row 3.

For a shorter (or longer) poncho, work fewer (or additional) Row 3 reps until reaching your desired length.

Fasten off.

Finishing Sleeve Openings

Attach yarn to the bottom of the armhole opening with a sl st.

Ch 1, sc evenly around armhole opening, working approximately 2 sc for every dc row-end, sl st into first sc to join rnd, fasten off.

Rep for second armhole.

Weave in any remaining ends.

Block your poncho to the dimensions listed in the Sizing Chart (page 39).

Row 27: Ch 1, dc into first dc in Section 2 and *dc in each dc until next Puff, sk Puff, (Puff, ch 2, Puff) into center ch2-sp from row below, sk next Puff; rep from * once more, dc in each st to end of row, ch 1, sl st into first dc from Row 27-Section 1 to join rnd, turn.

Rosebud
Cardigan

The Rosebud Cardigan is a timeless layering piece that will never go out of fashion and is sure to complement any outfit. Designed for both fashion and function, this cardigan features matching front pockets, an optional waist tie and short rows along the collar. For a breezy, casual look, wear it open and show off your outfit underneath. Fasten the waist tie for a cozy, fitted cardigan that will remain secure and hug your body, keeping you warm, or try adding buttons and buttonholes in place of the tie. The contrasting stitch pattern in the top few rows of the pockets provides a dynamic mix of textures without being distracting, unified by the monochromatic nature of this sweater. Pair with jeans and your favorite boots for a laid-back look.

Note: This cardigan is a variation on one of my all-time best-selling patterns, the Rosebud Raglan—a simple raglan pullover that matches this cardigan. The original Rosebud Raglan crochet pattern can be found on all pattern-selling platforms. For more information, visit knitsnknots.ca/rosebud-raglan.

Construction

The body of this cardigan is worked all in one piece, starting with the back panel, then splitting for two front panels that get folded over onto the back. The sleeves are worked directly onto the body in joined rounds, with tapered sleeves. The collar, pockets and waist tie are added last.

Materials

Yarn:
Worsted—Lion Brand Jeans in Top Stitch (100% acrylic)

246 yds (225 m) per 3.5-oz (100-g) skein

Find this yarn on lionbrand.com or visit yarnsub.com to find comparable substitutes.

Yardage:
6 (6, 7, 7, 8) (8, 9, 9, 9) skeins or 1350 (1425, 1550, 1675, 1800) (1850, 1975, 2050, 2150) yds [1235 (1304, 1418, 1532, 1646) (1692, 1806, 1875, 1966) m]

Note: Budget friendly!

Substitute Lion Brand Jeans with any worsted weight, category #4 yarn that matches gauge. Any fiber should work out fine. Jeans is one of my favorite budget-friendly yarns because it has a softness that is hard to find in acrylics within this price range.

Hook:
Size U.S. I/9 (5.5 mm) or size needed to obtain gauge

Notions:
Tapestry needle, several locking stitch markers, buttons (optional)

Gauge:
4 x 4" (10 x 10 cm) = 12 sts and 12 rows in stitch pattern (see instructions below)

Ch 15.

Row 1: Sc in 2nd ch from hook, dc in next ch, *sc in next ch, dc in next ch; rep from * to end of row, turn. [14 sts]

Row 2: Ch 1, sc in first dc, dc in next sc, *sc in next dc, dc in next sc; rep from * to end of row, turn.

Rep Row 2 until you have 15 rows worked.

Block your swatch. Measure the inner 4 inches (10 cm) of your blocked swatch to get the most accurate measurement.

ABBREVIATIONS
Written in U.S. crochet terms
ch: chain
cont in patt: continue in pattern (this means to sc in every dc and dc in every sc)
dc: double crochet
FSC: foundation single crochet (see Foundation Stitches in the Techniques section on page 172)
PM: place marker
rep: repeat
rnd: round
sc: single crochet
sc2tog: single crochet 2 stitches together
sk: skip
sl st: slip stitch
st(s): stitch(es)
tch: turning chain

Schematic

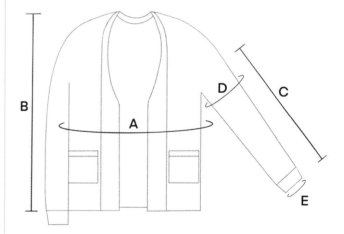

Rosebud Sizing Chart

	A FINISHED BUST CIRCUMFERENCE	B TOTAL LENGTH MEASURED FROM TOPS OF SHOULDERS TO BOTTOM OF CARDIGAN	C SLEEVE LENGTH MEASURED FROM UNDERARM	D UPPER ARM CIRCUMFERENCE	E WRIST CIRCUMFERENCE
XS	36" 91 cm	23" 58 cm	21" 53 cm	11.25" 29 cm	8" 20 cm
S	40" 102 cm	23" 58 cm	20.5" 52 cm	12" 30 cm	8" 20 cm
M	44" 112 cm	23" 58 cm	19.5" 50 cm	12.75" 32 cm	8.75" 22 cm
L	48" 122 cm	23" 58 cm	18.75" 48 cm	13.25" 34 cm	8.75" 22 cm
XL	52" 132 cm	23" 58 cm	17.75" 45 cm	15.25" 39 cm	9.25" 23 cm
2X	56" 142 cm	23" 58 cm	17" 43 cm	16.75" 43 cm	9.25" 23 cm
3X	60" 152 cm	23" 58 cm	16" 41 cm	17.25" 44 cm	9.25" 23 cm
4X	64" 163 cm	23" 58 cm	15.25" 39 cm	20" 51 cm	10" 25 cm
5X	68" 173 cm	23" 58 cm	14.25" 36 cm	20" 51 cm	10" 25 cm

This chart shows the finished garment measurements. This sweater is designed to be worn with approximately 6 to 8 inches (15 to 20 cm) of positive ease. Find the finished bust measurement in this chart and choose a size that is 6 to 8 inches (15 to 20 cm) larger than your actual bust measurement. For reference, the model is 5 feet, 4 inches (163 cm) tall with a 34-inch (86-cm) bust and is wearing a size small with a finished garment bust measurement of 40 inches (102 cm) with 6 inches (15 cm) of positive ease. If between sizes, size up.

For more information and tester photos, visit knitsnknots.ca/rosebud-cardigan.

Rosebud Pattern

Back Panel

Row 1: FSC 54 (60, 66, 72, 78) (84, 90, 96, 102).

Row 2: Ch 1 (does not count as a st here and throughout), sc in first st, dc in next st, *sc in next st, dc in next st; rep from * to end of row, turn. [54 (60, 66, 72, 78) (84, 90, 96, 102) sts]

Row 3: Ch 1, sc in first dc, dc in next sc, *sc in next dc, dc in next sc; rep from * to end of row, turn.

Row 4–66: Rep Row 3.

For a longer (or shorter) cardigan, work additional (or fewer) rows until the back panel measures the desired length. Additional length will require more yarn than listed in the Materials section (page 43).

Do not fasten off, continue with working yarn to First Front Panel.

First Front Panel

Row 1: Ch 1, sc in first dc, *dc in next sc, sc in next dc; rep from * 10 (11, 13, 14, 16) (17, 19, 20, 22) more times, turn. [23 (25, 29, 31, 35) (37, 41, 43, 47) sts]

Row 2: Ch 1, sk first sc, *sc in next dc, dc in next sc; rep from * to end of row, turn. [22 (24, 28, 30, 34) (36, 40, 42, 46) sts]

Row 3: Ch 1, *sc in next dc, dc in next sc; rep from * to end of row, turn.

Row 4–72: Rep Row 3.

> *Note:* If you modified your back panel, work the same modification to your front panels.

Fasten off, leaving a 30-inch (76-cm) tail for seaming side of cardigan (or a longer tail if you added length to your cardigan).

Second Front Panel

Count 23 (25, 29, 31, 35) (37, 41, 43, 47) sts from unworked edge and attach new yarn with sl st into this st, leaving 8 (10, 8, 10, 8) (10, 8, 10, 8) sts from back panel unworked.

Row 1: Ch 1, dc in same sc as sl st, *sc in next dc, dc in next sc; rep from * to end of row, turn. [23 (25, 29, 31, 35) (37, 41, 43, 47) sts]

Row 2: Ch 1, *sc in next dc, dc in next sc; rep from * until 1 st remains, sk last st, turn. [22 (24, 28, 30, 34) (36, 40, 42, 46) sts]

Row 3: Ch 1, *sc in next dc, dc in next sc; rep from * to end of row, turn.

Row 4–73: Rep Row 3.

Fasten off, leaving a 30-inch (76-cm) tail for seaming side of cardigan (or a longer tail if you added length to your cardigan).

> *Note:* The Second Front Panel has one more row than the First Front Panel so that the tail is left in the correct position to seam the side of the cardigan. You won't notice this difference in the final piece, but if it bothers you to have this discrepancy of one row, you can work them both the same and use scrap yarn to seam the side.

Sleeves

Fold your front panels over the top of your Back Panel, lining up the Back Panel foundation row with the last rows from your front panels (the bottom of your cardigan) stitch-for-stitch as best you can. Follow the stitches up to the fold-line—the top edge where the front panel folds onto the back panel—and place a stitch marker on the outer edge of each side of the cardigan to mark the center-top of the shoulder where your sleeves will be worked. You will use this marker to establish the center point of the shoulders to properly position your sleeves. For reference, this center fold should occur somewhere near the third or fourth row of the front panel.

Pick one side of your cardigan to begin with. Turn your work sideways to begin crocheting the first sleeve row along the outer edge of the rows, with the st marker in the center. Count 17 (18, 19, 20, 23) (25, 26, 30, 30) rows toward the front panel from center marker and PM here. Count 16 (17, 18, 19, 22) (24, 25, 29, 29) rows toward the back panel from center marker and PM here to mark your starting point. This marker is where you will begin Row 1.

Note: Treat each row-end of the body panel as a st.

Row 1: Insert your hook into marked st on back panel, join with sl st into marked st, ch 1, sc in same st as sl st, dc in next row-end, *sc in next row-end, dc in next row-end, rep from * across, passing center marker, up to and including farthest marked st, bring your first and last st together to connect the sleeve, sl st into first st of row to join in the rnd, turn. [34 (36, 38, 40, 46) (50, 52, 60, 60) sts]

After Row 1, you can seam the sides of your cardigan with a tapestry needle to make it easier to work the rest of the sleeves if you prefer. See Seaming on page 49.

Note: Sleeves are worked in joined, turned rounds; when finishing a row, remember to sl st into the first st of the row to join in the round and then turn your work.

Notes: For tighter (or looser) sleeves, simply add (or omit) decrease rounds as you see fit.

For longer (or shorter) sleeves than measurements provided in the Sizing Chart on page 45, simply add or omit non-decrease rounds as you see fit.

For the remainder of the sleeve, work the rnds as specified for your size below:

When instructed to decrease, work the rnd as follows: Ch 1, sk first st, cont in patt until 1 st remains unworked, sk last st, sl st into first st to join rnd, turn. [Decreases rnd by 2 sts]

The first stitch of your row will alternate between a sc and a dc each time you decrease.

Every rnd that is NOT a decrease rnd is worked as follows: Ch 1, cont in patt to end of rnd, sl st into first st to join, turn.

Follow your size only; total number of rnds given includes Rnd 1 you just completed.

Size XS: Work a total of 57 rnds, decreasing in the following rnds: 10, 20, 30, 40, 50. [24 sts]

Size S: Work a total of 56 rnds, decreasing in the following rnds: 8, 16, 24, 32, 40, 48. [24 sts]

Size M: Work a total of 53 rnds, decreasing in the following rnds: 12, 19, 26, 33, 40, 47. [26 sts]

Size L: Work a total of 51 rnds, decreasing in the following rnds: 7, 14, 21, 28, 35, 42, 49. [26 sts]

Size XL: Work a total of 48 rnds, decreasing in the following rnds: 5, 10, 15, 20, 25, 30, 35, 40, 45. [28 sts]

Size 2X: Work a total of 45 rnds, decreasing in the following rnds: 4, 8, 12, 16, 20, 24, 28, 32, 36, 40, 44. [28 sts]

Size 3X: Work a total of 42 rnds, decreasing in the following rnds: 9, 12, 15, 18, 21, 24, 27, 30, 33, 36, 39, 42. [28 sts]

Size 4X: Work a total of 40 rnds, decreasing in the following rnds: 4, 6, 9, 11, 14, 16, 19, 21, 24, 26, 29, 31, 34, 36, 39. [30 sts]

Size 5X: Work a total of 37 rnds, decreasing in the following rnds: 4, 6, 9, 11, 14, 16, 19, 21, 24, 26, 29, 31, 34, 36. [32 sts]

Sleeve Cuff

Rnd 1: Ch 1, sc in each st around, sl st into first st to join, turn. [24 (24, 26, 26, 28) (28, 28, 30, 32) sc]

Rnd 2: Ch 1, sk first st, sc in next st and each st around until 1 st remains, sk last st, sl st into first st to join, turn. [22 (22, 24, 24, 26) (26, 26, 28, 30) sc]

Rnds 3–4: Rep Rnd 1–2. [20 (20, 22, 22, 24) (24, 24, 26, 28) sc]

Rnds 5–9: Rep Rnd 1.

Fasten off, weave in ends.

Rep all instructions for other sleeve.

Seaming

With a tapestry needle, use any remaining tails to seam the sides of your cardigan and close any gaps using the whip stitch (see Techniques on page 167) or seaming method of your choice, starting from the bottom and working your way up toward the sleeves. Rep for both sides.

Collar

Attach yarn to the bottom inside corner with a sl st to begin working along the cardigan's edge to create a collar. You will be working a few short rows to shape the collar.

Customization Tip: You can easily add buttons to this cardigan by placing stitch markers on the collar edge to mark out where you would like the buttons to be. I recommend working buttonholes on the fourth or fifth row so that a symmetrical number of rows exist before and after the buttonhole row. To create the buttonholes on one side of your sweater, follow the collar instructions as written, but skip over 1 to 3 stitches every time you approach a new stitch marker, and ch 1 to 3, depending on how many sts you skipped. (The size of these buttonholes depends on the size of the buttons you use.) On the following row, sc into each st and each ch, then continue the remainder of the pattern as written. Once the collar is completed, sew buttons in place on the opposite side of your sweater to line up with each buttonhole.

First Side Only

Row 1: [No tch] Work 1 sc into every row-end, stopping once you have reached approximately 4 inches (10 cm) higher than the center of your bust, PM into the edge of last st, turn.

Row 2: [No tch] Sk first sc, sc in next sc and each sc to end of row, turn.

Row 3: [No tch] Sc in each st across but stop 2 inches (5 cm) from end of row, PM into edge of last st, turn.

Row 4: Rep Row 2.

Row 5: Rep Row 3.

Row 6: Rep Row 2.

At this point, you should have 3 short rows completed. Each short row has a stitch marker at the end of your row to designate where you turned and skipped a st. The skipped stitch was to create a more subtle turn at the end of the row. To compensate for this missing stitch, in Row 7 you will place one new stitch into this marked space as you work one new row across all of your short rows.

Row 7: [No tch] Sc in each sc until reaching the first marker that designates the placement of the skipped stitch at the end of a short row. Work 1 sc into this marked row-end to make up for the skipped stitch. Proceed to sc into each sc until reaching the next marker, then repeat this process until you have worked past all markers. Continue to sc up around the neckline, and back down the opposite side of the cardigan until reaching the opposite bottom corner, turn.

Second Side Only

You now have 7 rows completed on one side of the collar, and 1 row completed on the second side. You will continue working over the second side only. You will start with Row 2 because you have just completed one row (Row 7 of First Side also becomes Row 1 of Second Side).

Row 2: [No tch] Work 1 sc into each sc, stopping once you have reached approximately 4 inches (10 cm) higher than the center of your bust, PM into the edge of your last st, turn.

Row 3: [No tch] Sk first sc, sc in next sc and each sc to end of row, turn.

Row 4: [No tch] Sc in each st across but stop 2 inches (5 cm) from end of row, PM into edge of last st, turn.

Row 5: Rep Row 3.

Row 6: Rep Row 4.

Row 7: Rep Row 3.

Row 8: [No tch] Sc in each sc until reaching the first marker that designates the placement of the skipped stitch at the end of a short row. Work 1 sc into this marked row-end to make up for the skipped stitch. Proceed to sc into each sc until reaching the next marker, then repeat this process until you have worked past all markers. Continue to sc up around the neckline, and back down the opposite side of the cardigan until reaching the opposite bottom corner, turn.

Both sides of your collar should now be symmetrical, with 8 rows completed.

Row 9–12: [No tch] Sc in each st to end of row, turn.

Customization Tip: For a wider collar, rep last row until it measures your desired collar width.

Fasten off once the desired width is achieved.

Optional Waist Tie

Row 1: FSC 138 (150, 162, 174, 186) (198, 210, 222, 234) or until reaching your desired waist tie length.

Using these numbers will create a tie that measures 46 (50, 54, 58, 62) (66, 70, 74, 78)" (117 [127, 137, 147, 157] [168, 178, 188, 198] cm) in length.

Row 2–8: Ch 1, sc in each st across, turn.

Fasten off.

Pocket (Make 2)

Note: The pocket is worked bottom-up, with some decreasing at the top to prevent sagging over time. When the top is stretched to the same width as the rest of the pocket, this helps keep the pocket opening taut against the front panel.

Row 1: FSC 20 (22, 26, 28, 30) (32, 34, 36, 38), leaving a 16-inch (41-cm) tail for seaming the pocket onto your cardigan.

Row 2: Ch 1, *sc in next st, dc in next st; rep from * to end of row, turn.

Row 3: Ch 1, *sc in next dc, dc in next sc; rep from * to end of row, turn.

Row 4–16: Rep Row 3.

For a deeper pocket, rep Row 3 until you have the desired pocket depth.

Next, you will work the contrasting border. Over time, pockets tend to lose their elasticity. The decreases in the next few rows will compensate for this in an attempt to help keep the pockets' shape over time.

Next Row: Ch 1, sc in each st across, turn.

Next Row: Ch 1, sc in first st, sc2tog, sc in next st and each st across until 3 sts remain, sc2tog, sc in last st, turn. [18 (20, 24, 26, 28) (30, 32, 34, 36) sc]

Next Row: Ch 1, sc in each st across, turn.

Rep last 2 rows. [16 (18, 22, 24, 26) (28, 30, 32, 34) sc]

Fasten off, leaving a 16-inch (41-cm) tail for seaming the pocket onto your cardigan. Block your pocket before seaming, if desired.

Attaching

Use stitch markers to temporarily place the pockets where desired. Stretch the top rows so that they are pinned to the same width as the rest of the pocket. Try on your cardigan to make sure you like the placement.

Note: Make sure your pockets are high enough to account for any stretching that may happen to your cardigan. If your chosen yarn will grow upon blocking or washing, or with wear, you will want to attach your pockets a little higher than your desired placement.

Once satisfied with their placement, use a tapestry needle and the two tails to sew your pockets onto the sweater along the perimeter of the bottom and both sides. See the Techniques section (page 178) for help with attaching pockets.

Customization Tip: To prevent your pockets from stretching out and losing their shape, you can sew a thin elastic to the inside of the pocket that measures slightly shorter than the width of your pocket. If you are not comfortable with sewing, you can also use a fabric glue to achieve similar results.

Weave in any remaining ends.

Block your cardigan to the dimensions listed in the Sizing Chart (page 45).

Snow Day

The Warmest Sweaters for the Coldest Days

For half of the year, my world looks like the inside of a snow globe. I've grown to appreciate the peacefulness of the winter season, which invites you to slow down and enjoy the moment—but more so for the ability to wear all of my sweaters that I spent most of the summer making. Even before I knew how to crochet, I loved chunky sweaters and the classic element they bring to any outfit.

All five patterns in this chapter produce chunky sweaters that look sophisticated and balanced. It can be challenging to create subtle designs with chunky yarn because crochet brings a unique challenge to garment design: drape. Crochet stitches are inherently bulky and lie differently than knitted stitches, meaning extra care must be taken when choosing the stitch pattern, hook and yarn used to achieve the desired fabric. A dense and heavy stitch pattern often creates unwanted structure in a garment and tends to compromise the drape we are trying to achieve, so I kept it light and airy to encourage the chunky yarn to flow beautifully on the body during wear.

In this chapter, you will find an eclectic mix of faux fur, a turtleneck, chunky yarn and oversized fits to perfectly blend fashion and function. I am drawn to natural, organic textures with a neutral color palette, and had a lot of fun experimenting with a variety of fibers in this chapter. Inspired by the timeless beauty of nature, each piece was created for the outdoors with snowy adventures in mind. Brave the winter in these stylish cool-weather staples.

Vintage Moon
Circular Yoke

No sweater collection would be complete without a turtleneck. Like a moth to a flame, I am constantly drawn to the polish of high necklines. There is a certain warmth and security that comes with a high neckline, an inherently sophisticated addition to any garment. Bringing style and function to this simple yoke sweater, the turtleneck radiates a classic elegance, like a fashion-forward nod to the past.

With its relaxed fit and slim, tapered sleeves, Vintage Moon can be comfortably worn under a parka, sheltering your neck from harsh winter winds. This sweater lands at the upper thigh (though you can adjust the length to suit your preference), and the sleeves extend slightly past the wrist for additional protection from the cold. This design feels warm and grounding, while adding a touch of poise to any outfit.

Construction

This sweater has a circular yoke construction, worked seamlessly from the top down after working the cowl ribbing. After completing the yoke increases, the yoke is then separated to create space for the body and the armholes. The body is worked next, and the sleeves are worked last. The benefit to this type of top-down construction is that you can try it on as you crochet it and make adjustments as necessary to ensure a perfect fit. This is especially helpful for discovering your desired sleeve and body length. The entire piece is worked in a spiral for a smooth, seamless fabric with no visible seams or joins.

Skill Level: Easy

Materials

Yarn:
Bulky—The Hook Nook Yummy in Olive You (80% acrylic, 20% wool)
185 yds (170 m) per 3.5-oz (100-g) ball
Find this yarn on thehooknooklife.com.

Yardage:
6 (6, 6, 7, 7) (8, 8, 8, 9) skeins or 950 (1000, 1075, 1150, 1250) (1300, 1400, 1475, 1550) yds [869 (915, 983, 1052, 1143) (1189, 1281, 1349, 1418) m]

Note: Budget friendly!
Substitute The Hook Nook Yummy with any bulky weight, category #5 yarn that matches gauge. This particular yarn feels lighter than other comparable category #5 yarns. An aran weight or heavy worsted may work well too.

Main gauge hook:
Size U.S. K/10½ (6.5 mm) or size needed to obtain gauge

Hook for cowl and sleeve cuffs:
Size U.S. J/10 (6 mm) or hook that is 0.5 mm smaller than main gauge hook

Notions:
Tapestry needle, six locking stitch markers

Gauge:
6 x 6" (15 x 15 cm) = 14 sts and 12 rows in half double crochet in the round using main gauge (larger) hook

ABBREVIATIONS
Written in U.S. crochet terms
BOR: beginning of round
ch: chain
hdc: half double crochet
hdc2tog: half double crochet 2 stitches together
inc: increase—work 2 half double crochets into designated stitch
PM: place marker
rep: repeat
rnd(s): round(s)
sc: single crochet
scBLO: single crochet in the back loop only
sk: skip
sl st: slip stitch
st(s): stitch(es)
tch: turning chain

Schematic

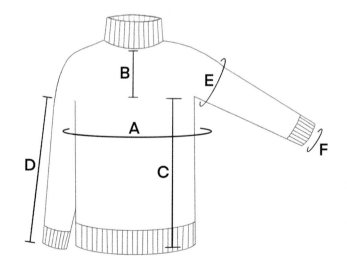

Vintage Moon Sizing Chart

	A FINISHED BUST CIRCUMFERENCE	**B** YOKE DEPTH MEASURED FROM FIRST ROUND TO LAST YOKE ROUND	**C** BODY LENGTH MEASURED FROM UNDERARM	**D** SLEEVE LENGTH MEASURED FROM UNDERARM	**E** UPPER ARM CIRCUMFERENCE	**F** WRIST CIRCUMFERENCE
XS	35" 89 cm	6.5" 17 cm	19" 48 cm	17.5" 44 cm	14.5" 37 cm	7.5" 19 cm
S	39.5" 100 cm	6.5" 17 cm	19" 48 cm	17.5" 44 cm	15" 38 cm	7.5" 19 cm
M	43" 109 cm	6.5" 17 cm	19" 48 cm	17.5" 44 cm	15.75" 40 cm	7.75" 20 cm
L	47" 119 cm	7" 18 cm	19" 48 cm	17.5" 44 cm	16.75" 43 cm	7.75" 20 cm
XL	51" 130 cm	7" 18 cm	19" 48 cm	17.5" 44 cm	18.5" 47 cm	8" 20 cm
2X	53" 135 cm	7" 18 cm	19" 48 cm	17.5" 44 cm	20" 51 cm	9" 23 cm
3X	59" 150 cm	7.5" 19 cm	19" 48 cm	17.5" 44 cm	21.75" 55 cm	9" 23 cm
4X	63" 160 cm	8.5" 22 cm	19" 48 cm	17.5" 44 cm	23" 58 cm	9.25" 23.5 cm
5X	67" 170 cm	8.5" 22 cm	19" 48 cm	17.5" 44 cm	23" 58 cm	9.25" 23.5 cm

This chart shows the finished garment measurements. This sweater is designed to be worn with approximately 5 to 7 inches (13 to 18 cm) of positive ease. When choosing a size, find the bust measurement in this chart that equals approximately 5 to 7 inches (13 to 18 cm) larger than your actual bust measurement and make this size. For reference, the model is 5 feet, 4 inches (163 cm) tall with a 34-inch (86-cm) bust and is wearing a size small with a finished garment bust measurement of 39.5 inches (100 cm). If between sizes, size down.

For more information and tester photos, visit knitsnknots.ca/vintage-moon.

Vintage Moon Pattern

Right Side: The "right side" is the side of your work that faces you as you crochet the yoke, body, and sleeves.

Turtleneck

Use a U.S. J/10 (6 mm) crochet hook or smaller hook.

Ch 34, leaving a 20-inch (51-cm) tail for seaming your turtleneck closed.

> *Customization Tip:* For a shorter or taller turtleneck than the sample shown, work fewer or additional chains here as you see fit. For reference, the turtleneck in the sample sweater measures approximately 10 inches (25 cm) before folding in half.

Row 1: Sc in 2nd ch from hook and in each ch to end of row, turn. [33 sc]

Row 2: Ch 1, sc in first st, scBLO to last st, sc last st, turn.

Rep Row 2 until you have a total of 60 (63, 63, 66, 69) (69, 69, 72, 72) rows.

Turn your work 90 degrees to begin working into the ends of the rows you just worked.

Set-Up Rnd: Ch 1, work 1 hdc into the ends of each row of ribbing, then bring your first and last st together to form a tube. Hdc straight into the first hdc to join your work and set yourself up to work in a spiral. [60 (63, 63, 66, 69) (69, 69, 72, 72) hdc]

Place a stitch marker in this last hdc to mark the center-back (BOR). Move this marker up every time you work each rnd.

With a tapestry needle, use the tail from your ch to seam the first and last rows of the turtleneck into a tube using the whip stitch (see Techniques on page 167) or seaming method of your choice.

Yoke

Switch to U.S. K/10½ (6.5 mm) crochet hook or main gauge (larger) hook.

Increase Rnd 1
*Inc in next st, hdc in next 2 sts; rep from * to end of rnd. [80 (84, 84, 88, 92) (92, 92, 96, 96) hdc]

Hdc in each st for next 2 (2, 2, 2, 2) (2, 1, 1, 1) rnds.

Increase Rnd 2
*Inc in next st, hdc in next 3 sts; rep from * to end of rnd. [100 (105, 105, 110, 115) (115, 115, 120, 120) hdc]

Hdc in each st for next 3 (3, 2, 3, 2) (2, 1, 2, 2) rnds.

Increase Rnd 3
Size XS: Hdc in first 5 sts, *hdc in next 4 sts, inc in next st; rep from * to last 5 sts, hdc in last 5 sts. [118 hdc]

All remaining sizes: *Inc in next st, hdc in next 4 sts; rep from * to end of rnd. [x (126, 126, 132, 138) (138, 138, 144, 144) hdc]

Hdc in each st for next 4 (4, 2, 2, 2) (2, 1, 1, 1) rnds.

Sizes XS and S are now finished with the yoke; skip to Separating Body & Sleeves. All remaining sizes continue to Increase Rnd 4.

Increase Rnd 4

M: Hdc in first 6 sts, *inc in next st, hdc in next 9 sts; rep from * to end of rnd. [138 hdc]

L: Hdc in first 6 hdc, *inc in next st, hdc in next 5 sts; rep from * to last 6 sts, hdc in last 6 sts. [152 hdc]

All remaining sizes: *Inc in next st, hdc in next 5 sts; rep from * to end of rnd. [x (x, x, x, 161) (161, 161, 168, 168) hdc]

Hdc in each st for next x (x, 2, 2, 1) (1, 1, 2, 2) rnds.

Size M and L are now finished with the yoke; skip to Separating Body & Sleeves. All remaining sizes continue to Increase Rnd 5.

Increase Rnd 5

XL: Hdc in first st, *inc in next st, hdc in next 39 sts; rep from * to end of rnd. [165 hdc]

All remaining sizes: *Inc in next st, hdc in next 6 sts; rep from * to end of rnd. [x (x, x, x, x) (184, 184, 192, 192) hdc]

Hdc in each st for next x (x, x, x, 1) (1, 2, 2, 2) rnds.

Size XL and 2X are now finished with the yoke; skip to Separating Body & Sleeves. All remaining sizes continue to Increase Rnd 6.

Increase Rnd 6

3X: Hdc in first 4 sts, *inc in next st, hdc in next 14 sts; rep from * to end of rnd. [196 hdc]

4X: Hdc in first 12 sts, *inc in next st, hdc in next 11 sts; rep from * to end of rnd. [207 hdc]

5X: *Inc in next st, hdc in next 7 sts; rep from * to end of rnd. [216 hdc]

Hdc in each st for next x (x, x, x, x) (x, 2, 2, 2) rnds.

At this point, your yoke should now have a total of 13 (13, 13, 14, 14) (15, 16, 17, 17) rnds completed.

Separating Body & Sleeves

Hdc in next 17 (19, 21, 23, 25) (28, 29, 31, 33) sts, ch 8 (9, 9, 9, 10) (10, 11, 12, 12), sk next 26 (26, 28, 30, 33) (37, 40, 42, 42) sts to create space for right sleeve, hdc in next 33 (37, 41, 46, 49) (55, 58, 61, 66) sts, ch 8 (9, 9, 9, 10) (10, 11, 12, 12), sk next 26 (26, 28, 30, 33) (37, 40, 42, 42) sts to create space for left sleeve, hdc in next 16 (18, 20, 23, 25) (27, 29, 31, 33) sts to BOR. [82 (92, 100, 110, 119) (130, 138, 147, 156) sts]

PM in first and last skipped st of each sleeve (2 markers per sleeve). You will need to refer to these markers when working the first sleeve round.

Body

BOR marker can now be removed.

Next Rnd: Hdc in each st and each ch to end of rnd.

Hdc in each st around until 4 inches (10 cm) shorter than your desired length.

Once you are satisfied with the length, find the approximate center of each underarm, follow directly down to the bottom of your sweater and place a marker in your last row of the body to mark the two placements of the split hem.

You are going to begin your bottom hem ribbing at one of the markers, so continue to hdc in each st until 6 sts away from next marker, sc in next 3 sts, sl st in next 3 sts.

You should now be at one of your marked sts.

Bottom Hem Ribbing
Continue with U.S. K/10½ (6.5 mm) crochet hook or main gauge (larger) hook.

Ch 13.

Row 1: Sc in 2nd ch from hook and in each ch across. [12 sc]

Find the st that the initial ch came out of. Do not work into this st, but sl st into the next 2 sts of the body. Turn work to begin working back on the previous row of sc.

Row 2: [No tch] Sk the 2 sl st just made, scBLO in each sc to last sc, sc into both loops of last sc, turn, do not work tch.

Row 3: [No tch] Sc through both loops of first sc, scBLO into each remaining sc to end of row, sl st into next 2 body sts, turn work to begin working back on previous row of sc.

Customization Tip: For a hem that continues around the entire bottom of your sweater without any splits, continue to rep Row 2 and 3 around the circumference of your sweater until reaching the starting point, then fasten off and seam the first and last rows together. Weave in ends.

Rep Rows 2 and 3 until you have worked your way to the second marker, finishing on a Row 3 rep. Here, you will create the split hem.

Ch 13, rep Rows 1–3, then rep Rows 2 and 3 until reaching first marker. Fasten off.

Sleeves

With U.S. K/10½ (6.5 mm) crochet hook or main gauge (larger) hook, attach new yarn (with right side facing) with a sl st at the approximate center of the underarm.

Rnd 1 (Set-Up Rnd): Ch 1, work 4 (4, 4, 4, 5) (5, 5, 6, 6) hdc evenly spaced before first marker, hdc in next 26 (26, 28, 30, 33) (37, 40, 42, 42) sleeve sts up to and including the second marker, work 4 (5, 5, 5, 5) (5, 6, 6, 6) hdc evenly spaced to end of rnd. [34 (35, 37, 39, 43) (47, 51, 54, 54) hdc]

Hdc directly into first hdc from Rnd 1 to begin working in a spiral, PM in this st to mark BOR.

For the remainder of the sleeve, work the rnds as specified for your size below:

For sizes XS, S, M, L, XL: When instructed to decrease, work rnd as follows: Hdc in first st, hdc2tog, hdc in each st to end of rnd. [Decreases rnd by 1 st]

For sizes 2X, 3X, 4X, 5X: A "double decrease rnd" is worked as follows: Hdc in first st, hdc2tog, hdc in each st until 3 sts remain unworked, hdc2tog, hdc in last st. [Decreases rnd by 2 sts]

Work all non-decrease rnds as follows: Hdc all sts.

Size XS: Work a total of 30 rnds while decreasing in the following rnds: 4, 8, 12, 16, 20, 24, 28, 30. [26 hdc]

Size S: Work a total of 30 rnds while decreasing in the following rnds: 3, 6, 9, 12, 15, 18, 21, 24, 27. [26 hdc]

Size M: Work a total of 30 rnds while decreasing in the following rnds: 3, 6, 9, 12, 15, 18, 21, 24, 27, 30. [27 hdc]

Size L: Work a total of 30 rnds while decreasing in the following rnds: 2, 5, 7, 10, 12, 15, 17, 20, 22, 25, 27, 30. [27 hdc]

Size XL: Work a total of 30 rnds while decreasing in the following rnds: 2, 4, 6, 8, 10, 12, 14, 16, 18, 20, 22, 24, 26, 28, 30. [28 hdc]

Size 2X: Work for a total of 28 rnds while working the following rnds as double decrease rnds: 3, 6, 9, 12, 15, 18, 21, 24. [31 hdc]

Size 3X: Work a total of 27 rnds, while working the following rnds as double decrease rnds: 2, 5, 7, 10, 12, 15, 17, 20, 22, 25. [31 hdc]

Size 4X and 5X: Work a total of 26 rnds, while working the following rnds as double decrease rnds: 2, 4, 7, 9, 12, 14, 17, 19, 22, 24, 26. [32 hdc]

Do not fasten off; continue with working yarn to work Cuff Ribbing.

Cuff Ribbing
Using U.S. J/10 (6 mm) crochet hook or smaller hook.

Ch 11.

Row 1: Sc into 2nd ch from hook and in each ch. [10 sc]

Find the st that the initial ch came out of. Do not work into this st, but sl st into the next 2 sts of the last sleeve rnd. Turn work to begin working back on the previous row of sc.

Row 2: [No tch] Sk the 2 sl st just made, scBLO in each sc to last sc, sc into both loops of last sc, turn.

Row 3: [No tch] Sc through both loops of first sc, scBLO into each remaining sc to end of row, sl st into next 2 sleeve sts, turn work to begin working back on previous row of sc.

Rep Rows 2 and 3 until you have worked your way around your entire cuff. With a tapestry needle, seam the first and last row of ribbing together using the whip stitch or seaming method of your choice. Fasten off and weave in ends.

Rep all instructions for the second sleeve.

Block your sweater to the dimensions listed in the Sizing Chart (page 57). Blocking will help your ribbing lie flat without curling.

Fifty Below
Color Block Pullover

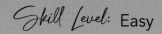

The Fifty Below Color Block Pullover is a cute, chunky sweater designed to be a part of all your winter adventures. Playfully plush and oh-so-cozy, this sweater is intended to stand out like a painting against the glistening white canvas of a snowy mountain. Inspired by the playful boldness of winter ski outfits that never hold back on color or style, this adorably unpretentious sweater is chock full of character from its quirky texture to the cheerful color blocking. The whimsical two-tone effect provides you with an opportunity to get creative and design your own color pattern. If ever there was a time to go crazy with color, it's right now, with this sweater. Fifty Below begs to be worn on your next snowy outing, and pairs best with ice skates or ski poles.

Construction

This pullover is worked in four pieces: a front panel, a back panel, and two sleeves. The front and back body panels are worked first and are partially seamed together along the shoulders and the sides, leaving openings for the sleeves to be attached. Next, the sleeves are worked flat from the wrist upward and are seamed closed before being attached to the body of the sweater. This pullover lands around the mid-hip, but instructions are included to easily make any length.

Notes: The ribbing used in this pattern differs from the ribbing techniques used throughout the rest of this book. See page 169 for help with this technique.

Follow along with the specified color changes to create a two-toned sweater like the sample shown or toss the rules aside to create your own color-blocking pattern by using whatever yarn you have on hand. Yardage has also been calculated for a solid color version for your convenience.

Materials

Yarn:
Bulky—Wool and the Gang Alpachino Merino in Chestnut Brown (Color A) and Sahara Dust (Color B) (60% Merino, 40% baby alpaca)
110 yds (100 m) per 3.5-oz (100-g) ball
Find this yarn on woolandthegang.com or visit yarnsub.com to find comparable substitutes.

Yardage (2-tone):
Color A (Bottom Color): 4 (5, 5, 5, 6) (7, 7, 7, 8) balls or 400 (450, 500, 550, 575) (675, 725, 750, 825) yds [366 (412, 458, 503, 526) (618, 663, 686, 755) m]
Color B (Top Color): 4 (4, 4, 5, 5) (6, 6, 7, 7) balls or 375 (400, 425, 475, 525) (575, 650, 700, 750) yds [343 (366, 389, 435, 481) (526, 595, 641, 686) m]
Yardage (solid color): 8 (8, 9, 10, 10) (12, 13, 14, 15) balls or 775 (850, 925, 1025, 1100) (1250, 1375, 1450, 1575) yds [709 (778, 846, 938, 1006) (1143, 1258, 1326, 1441) m]

Note: Budget-friendly alternatives include: The Hook Nook Yummy, Loops & Threads Cozy Wool. WeCrochet Biggo is also another great alternative for Alpachino Merino, though not quite as budget-friendly as some of the other options listed here.

Substitute Alpachino Merino with any other category #5, bulky-weight yarn that matches gauge. One of the reasons this yarn works so well in this sweater without feeling too heavy or dense is because it's composed of two slinky fibers—Merino wool and baby alpaca—that are gently twisted to create a fluffy, airy yarn.

Hook:
Size U.S. K/10½ (6.5 mm) or size needed to obtain gauge

Notions:
Tapestry needle, several locking stitch markers

(continued)

ABBREVIATIONS
Written in U.S. crochet terms
ch: chain

ch-sp: chain space

Yo-slst: Yarn-over slip stitch—Yarn over, insert hook into designated st, yarn over, draw loop through stitch and immediately through both loops on hook. This stitch is worked into the 3rd loop for most of the ribbing and is worked underneath the front and back loops at the beginning and end of the ribbing rows (see the Techniques section on page 169). Note that after turning your work to begin a new row, the 3rd loop appears in the front, and there should be two loops behind it that are left untouched to create a knit-like row of stitches on the opposite side of your work.

rep: repeat

rnd: round

sc: single crochet

sc2tog: single crochet 2 stitches together

sk: skip

sl st: slip stitch

st(s): stitch(es)

Gauge:
4 x 4" (10 x 10 cm) = 11.5 sts and 11 rows in granite stitch, where each sc counts as a stitch and each ch counts as a stitch (see instructions below)

Ch 15.

Row 1: Sc in 3rd ch from hook (note: skipped chs create 1 ch-sp), *ch 1, sk next ch, sc in next ch; rep from * to end of row, turn. [8 sc; 7 ch]

Row 2: Ch 2, sc in first ch-sp, *ch 1, sk next sc, sc in next ch-sp; rep from * to end of row, turn.

Rep Row 2 until you have at least 14 rows worked.

Block your swatch. Measure the inner 4 inches (10 cm) of your blocked swatch to get the most accurate measurement.

Note: The granite stitch has many names; it is often referred to as the linen stitch, seed stitch or moss stitch, to name just a few.

Schematic

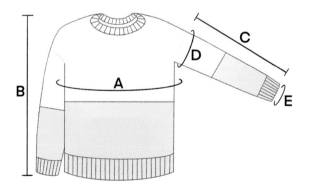

Fifty Below Sizing Chart

	A FINISHED BUST CIRCUMFERENCE	B TOTAL LENGTH MEASURED FROM TOPS OF SHOULDERS	C SLEEVE LENGTH MEASURED FROM UNDERARM	D UPPER ARM CIRCUMFERENCE	E WRIST CIRCUMFERENCE
XS	35.5" 90 cm	18" 46 cm	19.5" 50 cm	12" 30 cm	8.75" 22 cm
S	39.5" 100 cm	19.5" 49.5 cm	18.5" 47 cm	12" 30 cm	8.75" 22 cm
M	44" 112 cm	21" 53 cm	17.5" 44 cm	13.5" 34 cm	8.75" 22 cm
L	48" 122 cm	23" 58 cm	16.5" 42 cm	14.25" 36 cm	8.75" 22 cm
XL	52" 132 cm	24" 61 cm	15.5" 39 cm	15.75" 40 cm	9.5" 24 cm
2X	56" 142 cm	25.5" 65 cm	15" 38 cm	17.75" 45 cm	9.5" 24 cm
3X	60.5" 154 cm	27.5" 70 cm	13.5" 34 cm	19" 48 cm	9.5" 24 cm
4X	63.5" 161 cm	28.5" 72 cm	12.5" 32 cm	20.5" 52 cm	10" 25 cm
5X	67.5" 171 cm	30.5" 77 cm	11.5" 29 cm	20.5" 52 cm	10" 25 cm

This chart shows the finished garment measurements. This sweater is designed to be worn with approximately 6 to 8 inches (15 to 20 cm) of positive ease. Find the finished bust measurement in this chart, choose a size that is 6 to 8 inches (15 to 20 cm) larger than your actual bust measurement and make that size. For reference, the model is 5 feet, 4 inches (163 cm) tall with a 34-inch (86-cm) bust and is wearing a size small with a finished garment bust measurement of 39.5 inches (100 cm) with 5.5 inches (14 cm) of positive ease.

For more information and tester photos, visit knitsnknots.ca/fifty-below.

Fifty Below Pattern

Pattern Notes

Turning Chain: The turning chain for the granite stitch, the main stitch pattern (everything but the ribbing), counts as 1 sc + 1 ch and is included in the final stitch counts of each row.

Changing Colors Seamlessly: When working the last stitch of an old color, work the stitch as usual, but use the new color to do your final yarn-over and pull through to close the stitch. Then, you may cut the old color and continue stitching with the new color.

Front Panel

Bottom Ribbing

Using Color A and leaving a 24-inch (61-cm) tail for seaming the side of your sweater, ch 11.

Row 1: Yo-slst in 2nd ch from hook and in each ch across. [10 yo-slst]

Row 2: Ch 1 (does not count as a st here), yo-slst into front and back loops of first st, yo-slst into 3rd loop of next 8 sts, yo-slst into front and back loops of last st, turn.

Rep Row 2 until you have a total of 51 (57, 63, 69, 75) (81, 87, 91, 97) rows of ribbing completed. Do not turn your work after the last row.

Body

After the last row, turn your work to begin working into the edges of the rows you just completed.

Row 1: Ch 1, work 1 sc into the ends of each row you just completed, turn. [51 (57, 63, 69, 75) (81, 87, 91, 97) sc]

Row 2: Ch 2 (counts as 1 sc and 1 ch), sk first 2 sc, sc in third sc, *ch 1, sk next sc, sc in next sc; rep from * to end of row, turn. [26 (29, 32, 35, 38) (41, 44, 46, 49) sc]

Row 3: Ch 2, sc in first ch-sp, *ch 1, sk next sc, sc in next ch-sp; rep from * to end of row, turn.

Customization Tip: For a longer (or shorter) sweater than measurements provided in the Sizing Chart on page 65, add (or omit) rows as you see fit. To keep the color-blocking proportions consistent, you may want to add (or omit) rows in a multiple of two; one row for each of Color A and Color B. Note that working additional length will require additional yardage than listed in the Materials section (page 62).

Rep Row 3 until you have worked a total of 11 (13, 15, 17, 19) (21, 23, 25, 27) rows.

Switch to Color B and work an additional 24 (26, 28, 30, 32) (34, 36, 38, 40) rows.

You should now have a total of 35 (39, 43, 47, 51) (55, 59, 63, 67) rows completed.

Neckline

Side 1

Row 1: Ch 2, sc in first ch-sp, *ch 1, sk next sc, sc in next ch-sp; rep from * 9 (11, 12, 14, 15) (16, 17, 18, 20) more times, turn. [11 (13, 14, 16, 17) (18, 19, 20, 22) sc]

Row 2: Ch 2, sk first ch-sp, sk next sc, sc in next ch-sp, *ch 1, sk next sc, sc in next ch-sp; rep from * to end of row, turn. [10 (12, 13, 15, 16) (17, 18, 19, 21) sc]

Row 3: Ch 2, sc in first ch-sp, *ch 1, sk next sc, sc in next ch-sp; rep from * until 2 ch-sps remain, ch 1, sk next sc, sc2tog (working the last 2 ch-sps together), turn. [9 (11, 12, 14, 15) (16, 17, 18, 20) sc]

Row 4: Ch 2, sc in first ch-sp, *ch 1, sk next sc, sc in next ch-sp; rep from * to end of row, turn.

Rep Row 4 an additional 4 (5, 5, 6, 6) (6, 7, 7, 8) times.

At this point, you should have a total of 8 (9, 9, 10, 10) (10, 11, 11, 12) rows worked on Side 1.

Fasten off, leaving a 16-inch (41-cm) tail for seaming the shoulder.

Side 2

The second side will be worked the same as the first side. Starting at the opposite outer edge, attach new yarn to the corner ch-sp with a sl st. You will be working toward the center. Rep all instructions for Side 1. Fasten off, leaving a 16-inch (41-cm) tail for seaming the shoulder.

Back Panel

Rep all instructions from Front Panel until you have worked a total of 11 (13, 15, 17, 19) (21, 23, 25, 27) rows in Color A.

Switch to Color B and work an additional 32 (35, 37, 40, 42) (44, 47, 49, 52) rows.

You should now have a total of 43 (48, 52, 57, 61) (65, 70, 74, 79) rows completed.

Fasten off.

Partial Assembly

You are going to seam the shoulders and sides of the sweater before completing the sleeves. This way, you can try on your sweater and pin the sleeves in place as you work them to ensure the sleeves are the proper length for your arms before cutting your yarn and seaming the entire sweater together.

Lay the front panel over the top of the back panel, aligning the sides stitch-for-stitch with interlocking stitch markers starting from the bottom and working your way up. Arrange your panels so that the long tails you left from your beginning foundation chains are on opposite sides—the long tail from the back panel on one side, the long tail from the front panel on the other. These tails will be used to seam the sides of your sweater.

Starting from the bottom, using the long tails from the beginning chains, seam the sides of the sweater with a tapestry needle using the whip stitch (page 167) or seaming method of your choice, leaving plenty of space for attaching the sleeves later. You can seam your ribbing together first, then work your way back up to complete the sides of your sweater, or you can use a separate length of yarn to seam the ribbing if you prefer. Change colors where necessary. You will come back to this side seam, so don't fasten off yet. Rep for both sides.

To seam the tops of the shoulders, align the top rows of the front and back panels stitch-for-stitch with locking stitch markers to hold in place. With a tapestry needle and the tails left from your Front Panel Sides, seam the tops of the shoulders using the whip stitch or seaming method of your choice. Fasten off, weave in ends. Rep for both shoulders.

With a tapestry needle, seam the neckline ribbing closed using the whip stitch or seaming method of your choice and weave in all ends.

Sleeves (Make 2)

Customization Tip: If you have altered the specified rows of color blocking to create your own color blocking pattern or you want to ensure you have enough of Color A to complete both sleeves, take your remaining yarn of Color A and divide it evenly in half, one part for each sleeve. This way, you can get the most out of your yarn without running out on your second sleeve, and maybe even use up all of Color A without leaving any scraps.

Bottom Ribbing

Using Color A, ch 9, leaving a 24-inch (61-cm) tail for seaming your sleeve.

Row 1: Yo-slst in 2nd ch from hook and in each ch across, turn. [8 yo-slst]

Row 2: Ch 1, hdc sl st into front and back loops of first st, yo-slst into 3rd loop of next 6 sts, yo-slst into front and back loops of last st, turn.

Rep Row 2 until you have a total of 25 (25, 25, 25, 27) (27, 27, 29, 29) rows of ribbing completed.

After completing your last row, bring your first and last rows together to form a tube. Sl st into both layers of fabric across all 8 sts to seam your cuff closed.

Turn your work to begin working into the edges of the rows you just completed.

Row 1: Ch 1, work 1 sc into the ends of each row you just completed, turn. [25 (25, 25, 25, 27) (27, 27, 29, 29) sc]

Neckline Finishing

Using Color B, attach yarn to the neckline at one of the shoulder seams. Ch 1, sc around neckline as evenly as you can to create a set-up rnd for the ribbing, sl st into first sc to join.

Ch 4.

Row 1: Yo-slst in 2nd ch from hook through the top two loops, yo-slst into the 3rd loop of the next 2 ch, sl st in next 2 sts of set-up rnd, turn. [3 yo-slst]

Row 2: Ch 1, skip the 2 sl st just worked, yo-slst into the 3rd loop of the next 2 sts, yo-slst in last st, turn.

Row 3: Ch 1, yo-slst in first st through the top two loops, yo-slst into the 3rd loop of the next 2 sts, sl st in next 2 sts of set-up rnd, turn.

Rep Rows 2 and 3 until reaching starting point, fasten off.

Row 2: Ch 2, sk first 2 sc, sc in third sc, *ch 1, sk next sc, sc in next sc; rep from * to end of row, turn. [13 (13, 13, 13, 14) (14, 14, 15, 15) sc]

For the remainder of the sleeve, work the rows as specified for your size below:

When instructed to increase, work the row as follows: Ch 2, sk first sc, (sc, ch 1, sc) in first ch-sp, *ch 1, sk next sc, sc in next ch-sp; rep from * to end of row, turn. [increases row by 1 sc and 1 ch]

Every row that is NOT an increase row is worked as follows: Ch 2, sc in first ch-sp, *ch 1, sk next sc, sc in next ch-sp; rep from * to end of row, turn. (no increase)

Follow your size only; total number of rows given includes the 2 rows just completed.

Size XS: Work a total of 47 rows, increasing in the following rows: 3, 4, 20, 29, 40. Change to Color B after Row 20; leave 20-inch (51-cm) tails from each color for seaming the sleeve to the body. [18 sc]

Size S: Work a total of 44 rows, increasing in the following rows: 3, 4, 15, 24, 35. Change to Color B after Row 20; leave 20-inch (51-cm) tails from each color for seaming the sleeve to the body. [18 sc]

Size M: Work a total of 41 rows, increasing in the following rows: 3, 4, 9, 16, 23, 30, 37. Change to Color B after Row 20; leave 20-inch (51-cm) tails from each color for seaming the sleeve to the body. [20 sc]

Size L: Work a total of 39 rows, increasing in the following rows: 3, 4, 10, 15, 20, 25, 30, 35. Change to Color B after Row 20; leave 20-inch (51-cm) tails from each color for seaming the sleeve to the body. [21 sc]

Size XL: Work a total of 36 rows, increasing in the following rows: 3, 4, 7, 12, 15, 20, 23, 28, 31. Change to Color B after Row 18; leave 20-inch (51-cm) tails from each color for seaming the sleeve to the body. [23 sc]

Size 2X: Work a total of 34 rows, increasing in the following rows: 3, 4, 6, 9, 12, 15, 18, 21, 24, 27, 30, 33. Change to Color B after Row 18; leave 20-inch (51-cm) tails from each color for seaming the sleeve to the body. [26 sc]

Size 3X: Work a total of 30 rows, increasing in the following rows: 3, 4, 7, 8, 11, 12, 15, 16, 19, 20, 23, 24, 27, 28. Change to Color B after Row 18; leave 20-inch (51-cm) tails from each color for seaming the sleeve to the body. [28 sc]

Size 4X: Work a total of 28 rows, increasing in the following rows: 3, 4, 6, 7, 9, 10, 12, 13, 15, 16, 18, 19, 21, 22, 24. Change to Color B after Row 16; leave 20-inch (51-cm) tails from each color for seaming the sleeve to the body. [30 sc]

Size 5X: Work a total of 25 rows, increasing in the following rows: 3, 4, 6, 7, 9, 10, 12, 13, 15, 16, 18, 19, 21, 22, 24. Change to Color B after Row 16; leave long tails from each color for seaming the sleeve to the body. [30 sc]

Fasten off.

At this point, you may want to block your sleeves to smooth out any noticeable increases before seaming the length of your sleeve closed. With a tapestry needle, use your beginning tails to seam the length of the sleeves closed. Use Color A to seam the Color A sections and use Color B to seam the Color B sections.

Lay your sleeves in place with the seam at the bottom (toward the underarm). Use stitch markers to align each sleeve onto the body. Make sure to stretch the sleeve over the body sts slightly (approximately an inch [2.5 cm]) to avoid a tight sleeve seam.

With a tapestry needle and the tail you left after finishing the sleeve, seam the sleeves to the body with a matching color using the whip stitch or seaming method of your choice. Make sure to do this loosely and do not pull your yarn tight as you stitch, otherwise, the seam will feel tight and restricting. You want your seams to be loose so that your sleeve openings have some stretch just like the rest of the sweater.

Return to the side seams you stitched earlier to close any remaining gaps at the underarm.

Weave in any remaining ends, and block your sweater to the dimensions listed in the Sizing Chart (page 65).

Wandering Willow
Faux Fur Capelet

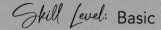

Skill Level: Basic

Reminiscent of the majestic winter outfits often shown in historical movies with castles and Vikings, this capelet will transport you to a simpler time with its vintage, old-world feel. Think of Wandering Willow as a wearable piece of art that will add depth and soul to any outfit: a statement piece that you proudly created yourself. You'll love the feeling of crocheting with these soft, furry stitches, and the way each stitch blends together to give the appearance of one continuous piece of plush fabric. Faux fur yarn pushes the limits on what we thought was possible to create with a crochet hook, and every fiber enthusiast needs to try this novelty yarn at least once.

Note: The magic of this design is that only one size is needed due to the gathering of the excess fabric created by the increases, and you can make a capelet of any length by continuing these simple increases for as many rounds as you like. You can also skip the closure at the neck and wear this piece as a shawl or a wrap if you prefer.

Construction

This capelet is worked from the top down in a circular yoke construction using only double crochet stitches, adding 12 stitches each row, until your desired capelet length.

Materials

Yarn:
Super Bulky—WeCrochet Fable Fur in Falke (100% polyester)

71 yds (65 m) per 3.5-oz (100-g) skein

Find this yarn on crochet.com or visit yarnsub.com to find comparable substitutes.

Yardage:
8 skeins or 525 yds (480 m)

Note: Budget friendly!

Substitute WeCrochet Fable Fur with another bulky, category #6 faux fur yarn that matches gauge. There are many other brands of faux fur on the market that would work great. You can, of course, make this pattern in a non–faux fur yarn, but it will not turn out to be a solid fabric like the sample shown.

Using a regular yarn will produce really defined stitches and probably some gaps between the double crochet stitches—but if you are okay with that then by all means use whatever yarn you'd like! (It might look amazing—there's only one way to find out!) Also note that eyelash yarn sometimes has the appearance of faux fur when it is wound up in a ball, but upon closer inspection, each strand is thin and wispy, and multiple strands must be held together as one to achieve a comparable fabric thickness. Make sure the fiber you choose is a bulky, category #6 faux fur yarn for a capelet similar to the sample shown in the photos.

Note: When working with faux fur yarn, your stitches will disappear into one smooth fabric and be difficult to distinguish. Use your fingers to feel for the next stitch, and simply add or skip a stitch if you realize your count is off by a stitch or two when you finish a row. Any minor mistakes like this will be hidden in your sea of fur stitches.

(continued)

Hook:

Size U.S. L/11 (8 mm) hook or size needed to obtain gauge

Note: In an oversized piece like this, gauge is less important. Use this recommended hook or choose whichever hook achieves your desired fabric density.

Notions:

Tapestry needle, twelve locking stitch markers
Optional—large toggle, button, ribbon, thread for closure

Note: You will use locking stitch markers to help keep track of your repeats by placing a marker in the second stitch of every increase. This will make it significantly easier to count your stitches or double-check your work as these stitches will all blend together into one smooth fabric and be difficult to distinguish. This will be especially helpful once you progress through the pattern and the rows have hundreds of stitches to count.

Gauge:

4 x 4" (10 x 10 cm) = 5 sts and 4 rows in double crochet

Schematic

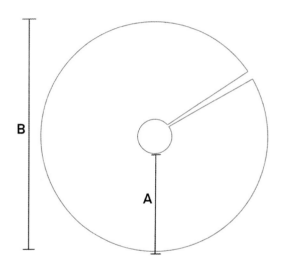

A. Beginning chain to Row 22 = 22" (56 cm)

B. Total diameter/width (measured flat) = 46" (117 cm)

For more information and tester photos, visit knitsnknots. ca/wandering-willow.

Wandering Willow Pattern

Ch 26.

Row 1: Dc in 3rd ch from hook and in each ch across, turn. [24 dc]

Row 2: Ch 2 (does not count as a st here and throughout), dc in first st, inc in next st, PM in second st of inc, *dc in next st, inc in next st, PM in second st of inc; rep from * to end of row, turn. [36 dc]

Row 3: Ch 2, inc in marked st, move marker up to second st of inc, *dc in each st to next marked st, inc in marked st, move marker up to second st of inc; rep from * across row until you have increased in your last marked st, dc in each st to end of row, turn. [48 dc]

Row 4: Ch 2, *dc in each st to next marked st, inc in marked st, move marker up to second st of inc; rep from * across row until you have increased in your last marked st, dc in each st to end of row, turn. [60 dc]

Rep Row 4 until desired length.

Sample shown has 22 rows, finishing with 276 dc in final row.

Fasten off, and weave in any remaining ends.

When you are satisfied with the size of your capelet, attach a toggle or large button as a closure. With a tapestry needle and faux fur yarn (or thread), sew on your toggle (or button) at the top corner where the tail is from your beginning chain, essentially joining the first and last stitches of Row 1. You could also use a fabric ribbon to weave through your first row of sts and tie a bow to close your capelet instead.

Customization Tip: If you would like to create armholes in this capelet for more of a cardigan style, you can do so with one simple step: Try on your capelet and stretch your arms out to the sides so they are parallel to the ground. Position the capelet to lie on your body the way you like to wear it, and then use locking stitch markers to grab the fabric on either side of your arm at the edge of the capelet, creating an arm hole. Use a scrap piece of matching yarn to make a secure knot here, and do the same to the opposite arm, then weave in your ends. Alternatively, you can also work one more row of double crochets, skipping over the fabric you gathered for the armholes.

Maple Grove
Cardigan

Inspired by the cold, winter days that beg you to curl up by the fire, my goal was to create a stylish garment that embodies the warmth and coziness of your favorite blanket or comfy robe. I consider this to be a wardrobe staple for the homebodies—somewhat of an informal, everyday piece.

Utilizing a mix of single crochet stitches and chain spaces, the granite stitch creates an unstructured, airy fabric that flows beautifully as it follows your movement. Landing just below the knee, this duster cardigan lends a sleek, lengthening effect to any outfit. The slim-fitting sleeves combined with a neat-looking collar and hem help balance the relaxed, boxy fit. These finishing details add sophistication while maintaining the dramatic, oversized vibe that we love so much.

Construction

This long cardigan is worked in granite stitch and features fold-over sleeve cuffs and optional afterthought pockets. The entire design is worked flat in one piece, then folded in half and seamed together at the end. A simple border is worked along the collar and bottom hem to clean up the edges, and optional pockets are sewn on last.

Materials

Yarn:
Worsted—Lion Brand Vanna's Choice in Oatmeal (92% acrylic, 8% rayon)
145 yds (133 m) per 3-oz (85-g) skein
Find this yarn on lionbrand.com or visit yarnsub.com to find comparable substitutes.

Yardage:
10 (11, 13, 14, 15) skeins or 1350 (1550, 1775, 2025, 2175) yds [1234 (1417, 1623, 1852, 1989) m]

Note on Yardage: Different colorways of Vanna's Choice have varying yardage. Make sure to check the yardage listed on the label of your desired colorway.

Note: Budget friendly!
Substitute Lion Brand Vanna's Choice with any medium-weight, category #4 yarn that matches gauge. Just note that certain fibers, are heavier than the one shown and will stretch more over time. You can compensate for this by working your cardigan slightly shorter than your desired length.

Main gauge hook:
Size U.S. K/10½ (6.5 mm) or size needed to obtain gauge

Hook for border:
Size U.S. G/7 (4.5 mm) hook or 2 sizes smaller than main gauge hook

Notions:
Tapestry needle, several locking stitch markers

Gauge:
4 x 4" (10 x 10 cm) = 14 sts and 10.5 rows in granite stitch (each sc counts as a stitch and each ch also counts as a stitch; see instructions below)
Using U.S. K/10½ (6.5 mm) crochet hook or main gauge (larger) hook.
Ch 19.

Row 1: Sc in 3rd ch from hook (note: skipped chs create 1 ch-sp), *ch 1, sk next ch, sc in next ch; rep from * to end of row, turn. [10 sc; 9 ch-sp]

Note: Final sc of each row is placed into ch-sp created from tch of previous row.

Row 2: Ch 2, sc in first ch-sp, *ch 1, sk next sc, sc in next ch-sp; rep from * to end of row, turn. [10 sc; 9 ch-sp]

Rep Row 2 until you have at least 13 rows worked.

Block your swatch. Measure the inner 4 inches (10 cm) of your swatch to get the most accurate measurement.

If you are having trouble achieving both stitch gauge and row gauge, choose the hook size that gives you the closest **stitch** gauge.

ABBREVIATIONS
Written in U.S. crochet terms
ch: chain
ch-sp: chain space
PM: place marker
rep: repeat
sc: single crochet
sc2tog: single crochet 2 stitches together
sk: skip
sl st: slip stitch
st(s): stitch(es)
tch: turning chain

Schematic

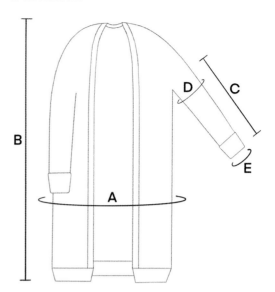

Maple Grove Sizing Chart

	A FINISHED BUST CIRCUMFERENCE	B TOTAL LENGTH MEASURED FROM TOPS OF SHOULDERS TO BOTTOM HEM	C SLEEVE LENGTH MEASURED FROM UNDERARM (UNCUFFED)	D UPPER ARM CIRCUMFERENCE	E WRIST CIRCUMFERENCE
XS	40" 102 cm	41" 104 cm	22" 56 cm	11.5" 29 cm	9" 23 cm
S/M	48" 122 cm	41" 104 cm	21.25" 54 cm	12" 30 cm	9.5" 24 cm
L/XL	56" 142 cm	41" 104 cm	20.5" 52 cm	15" 38 cm	9.5" 24 cm
2X/3X	64" 163 cm	41" 104 cm	19.75" 50 cm	19" 48 cm	10" 25 cm
4X/5X	68" 173 cm	41" 104 cm	19.75" 50 cm	20" 51 cm	10" 25 cm

This chart shows the finished garment measurements. This cardigan is intended to be worn with 10 to 16 inches (25 to 41 cm) of positive ease. When choosing a size, find the bust measurement in this chart that is closest to 10 to 16 inches (25 to 41 cm) larger than your actual bust measurement and make that size. For reference, the model is 5 feet, 4 inches (163 cm) tall with a 34-inch (86-cm) bust and is wearing a size S/M with a finished garment bust measurement of 48 inches (122 cm) worn with 14 inches (35 cm) of positive ease. If between sizes, size down.

For more information and tester photos, visit knitsnknots.ca/maple-grove.

Maple Grove Pattern

Pattern Notes

Turning Chain: The turning chain (ch-2) counts as 1 single crochet and 1 chain throughout the entire pattern and is included in the final stitch counts of each row and at each stitch count checkpoint.

Note: The granite stitch has many common names; it is often referred to as the linen stitch, seed stitch, mesh stitch, or moss stitch, to name a few.

Sizing: This sweater is written in five sizes as follows: XS (S/M, L/XL, 2X/3X, 4X/5X). Make sure to follow the numbers for your size only.

Back Panel

Use a U.S. K/10½ (6.5 mm) crochet hook or main gauge (larger) hook.

Ch 69 (83, 97, 111, 117).

Row 1: Sc in 3rd ch from hook (note: skipped chs count as 1 sc and 1 ch-sp), *ch 1, sk next ch, sc in next ch; rep from * to end of row, turn. [35 (42, 49, 56, 59) sc]

Row 2: Ch 2 (counts as 1 sc and 1 ch here and throughout), sk first sc, sc in first ch-sp, *ch 1, sk next sc, sc in next ch-sp; rep from * to end of row, turn.

> *Note:* Final sc of each row is placed into ch-sp created from tch of previous row.

Rep Row 2 until back panel measures 39 inches (99 cm) or until 2.25 inches (6 cm) shorter than your desired length. When determining your final length, be mindful that this stitch is known to grow (stretch) quite a bit in length after blocking and with wear.

Do not fasten off, continue with working yarn to First Front Panel.

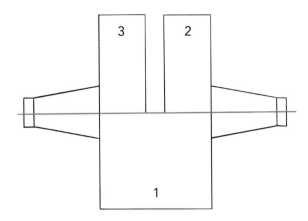

Figure 1: The body of Maple Grove is worked as one piece. The Back Panel (1) is worked first from the bottom up (to the red line). Next, the First Front Panel (2) is worked directly onto the Back Panel, then the Second Front Panel (3) is added to the opposite side in the same way. The red line also indicates the fold-line.

Front Panels

First Front Panel

Row 1: Ch 2, sk first sc, sc in first ch-sp, *ch 1, sk next sc, sc in next ch-sp; rep from * until you have worked a total of 15 (18, 22, 25, 27) sc, sc2tog, turn. [16 (19, 23, 26, 28) sc]

Row 2: Ch 2, sk first sc, sc2tog, *ch 1, sk next sc, sc in next ch-sp; rep from * to end of row, turn. [15 (18, 22, 25, 27) sc]

Row 3: Ch 2, sk first sc, sc in first ch-sp, *ch 1, sk next sc, sc in next ch-sp; rep from * to end of row, turn.

Rep Row 3 until the front panel measures the same as your back panel. Finish with an even-numbered row, ending on the outer edge of your work rather than the center.

Fasten off, leaving a long tail for seaming at the end.

Second Front Panel

The second panel will be worked the same as the first panel. Starting at the opposite outer edge, attach new yarn to the unworked corner with a sl st. You will be working toward the center.

Row 1: Ch 2, sk edge of next row, sc into edge of next row, *ch 1, sk edge of next row, sc into edge of next row; rep from * until you have worked a total of 20 (21, 26, 33, 35) sc, turn.

You can remove the marker at this point.

Row 2: Ch 2, sk first sc, sc in first ch-sp, *ch 1, sk next sc, sc in next ch-sp; rep from * to end of row, turn.

For the remainder of the sleeve, work the rows as specified for your size as follows:

When instructed to decrease, work the row as follows: Ch 2, sk first sc, sc in first ch-sp, ch 1, sk next sc, sc2tog over next 2 ch-sp, *ch 1, sk next sc, sc in next ch-sp; rep from * to end of row, turn. [decreases row by 1 sc and 1 ch]

Customization Tip: For tighter (or looser) sleeves, work additional (or fewer) decrease rows than instructed for your size. For longer (or shorter) sleeves, work additional (or fewer) non-increase rounds wherever you see fit. Make note of any modifications so that you can create a second identical sleeve.

Note: Total rnds provided include the first two rnds you have already completed.

Rep all instructions for First Front Panel until second panel measures the same length as the first panel. Finish with an even-numbered row, ending on the outer edge of your work rather than the center.

Fasten off, leaving a long tail for seaming at the end.

Sleeves

Lay your work flat and PM at the edge stitch of the last row of the back panel before splitting for the front panels to mark the center placement of each sleeve.

From this marker, count 19 (20, 25, 32, 34) rows toward front panel. Attach yarn to the edge stitch of this row with a sl st. You will be working toward the marker, counting the edge of each row as a st.

Size XS and S/M: Rep Row 2 until you have worked a total of 58 (56) rows, decreasing in the following rows: 12, 25, 36, 49. [16 (17) sc]

Size L/XL: Rep Row 2 until you have worked a total of 54 rows, decreasing in the following rows: 5, 10, 15, 20, 25, 30, 35, 40, 45. [17 sc]

Size 2X/3X: Rep Row 2 until you have worked a total of 52 rows, decreasing in the following rows: 3, 6, 9, 12, 15, 18, 21, 24, 27, 30, 33, 36, 39, 42, 45. [18 sc]

Size 4X/5X: Rep Row 2 until you have worked a total of 52 rows, decreasing in the following rows: 3, 6, 9, 12, 15, 18, 21, 24, 27, 30, 33, 36, 39, 42, 45, 48, 51. [18 sc]

Fasten off, leaving a 30-inch (76-cm) tail for seaming the sleeve closed.

Rep all instructions for the second sleeve.

Blocking

Before seaming the cardigan together, you may want to block your work to help smooth out any obvious decreases in the sleeves and help make your stitches appear more uniform.

Assembly

Fold the front panels over the back panel, aligning the first row of the back panel with the last row of the front panels. With a tapestry needle, use the long tails left from the front and back panels to seam the sides of the cardigan (see red lines in Figure 2) and use the long tails left from the last row of the sleeves to seam the sleeves (see blue lines in Figure 2) using the whip stitch (see Techniques on page 167) or seaming method of your choice. Fold sleeve cuffs up to desired height. Weave in ends.

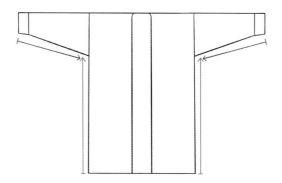

Figure 2: This diagram shows how to seam your cardigan together. Seam the sides along the red lines, starting from the bottom and working toward the underarm. Seam the sleeves along the blue lines, starting at the cuff, seaming toward the underarm, closing any remaining gaps at the underarm before fastening off and weaving in your ends.

Finishing

Using U.S. G/7 (4.5 mm) crochet hook or smaller gauge hook

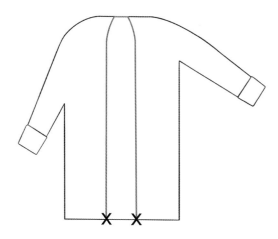

Figure 3: This diagram shows where to work the collar. Attach yarn to one of the bottom corners, denoted with an X. Work the remainder of the collar along the red line, ending at the opposite X.

Collar

Attach new yarn with sl st at one of the bottom inside corners (denoted in the diagram with an X) to begin working the collar.

Row 1: Ch 1, sc along inner edge of front panel, working 1 sc into the edge of each row until reaching the opposite bottom inside corner, turn.

Row 1 begins at one of the Xs. Next you will single crochet up and around the neckline along the red line until reaching the opposite bottom X. Here, you will turn and work back on the row you just created.

Rows 2–6: Ch 1, sc in each sc to end of row, turn.

Do not fasten off, continue with working yarn to Bottom Hem.

Bottom Hem

After completing the collar, you will work along the bottom edge of the cardigan (continuing with the smaller gauge hook).

Row 1: Ch 1, sc evenly into each sc and each ch along bottom edge until reaching the opposite corner, turn.

Customization Tip: For a tighter bottom hem, sk every 10th–15th st when working Row 1. This will prevent any flaring.

Row 2–6: Ch 1, sc in each sc to end of row, turn.

Fasten off, weave in all ends and block your sweater to the dimensions listed in the Sizing Chart (page 76).

Optional Pocket

Using U.S. K/10½ (6.5 mm) crochet hook or main gauge (larger) hook

Work an odd number of chs until reaching your desired pocket width.

Follow instructions from Row 1 and Row 2 of the Back Panel. Rep Row 2 until the pocket measures 1 inch (2.5 cm) shorter than your desired pocket depth.

Pocket Border
Use U.S. G/7 (4.5 mm) crochet hook or smaller hook.

Next Row: Ch 1, sc in each st across, turn.

Rep previous row until edging measures approximately 1 inch (2.5 cm).

Fasten off, leaving a long tail for seaming the pocket onto your cardigan.

Block your pocket if desired.

To attach the pocket, try on your finished cardigan and use stitch markers to mark your desired pocket placement. Keep in mind your cardigan may stretch slightly during wear, so you may want to place your pocket up to approximately 3 inches (8 cm) higher than your marked location. Lay your pocket flat in your desired location and pin it in place using stitch markers. With a tapestry needle, use the long tail to seam the pocket on to the cardigan. For more details on attaching your pocket, see the Techniques section on page 178.

Tip: When sewing pockets onto a cardigan, my preferred method is to insert the needle from top-to-bottom through the pocket and front panel of cardigan with the right side facing. Then, insert the needle from bottom-to-top, sewing through both layers. Rep this method all around the perimeter of the pocket, then fasten off and weave in ends once completed.

Rep all pocket instructions for any additional pockets.

Whispering Pines
Raglan

Named after the beautifully eerie sound heard when the winter wind breathes through the tall pine trees, Whispering Pines embodies the majestic nature of the woods. The solid, textured fabric resembles the density of a forest; the tall, slender trees echo in the slim fit of the sleeves. Despite being one of the more challenging patterns in this book, Whispering Pines is an approachable, unpretentious design. While there are no visually complex elements to this classic sweater, it somehow feels sophisticated and intricate. This sweater is insulating yet breathable, designed with winters in mind. Whether you're huddling around the campfire or catching up over lattes with your loved ones, this nature-inspired staple is sure to become a beloved favorite.

Construction

Whispering Pines features raglan shaping, worked seamlessly from the top down. After completing the yoke increases, short rows are added to the back edge to improve the fit, then the yoke is separated to create space for the body and the sleeves. The body is worked next, and the sleeves are worked last. The neckline ribbing at the collar can be worked at any point.

Materials

Yarn:
Aran/heavy worsted—WeCrochet City Tweed Aran in Toad (55% Merino wool, 25% superfine alpaca, 20% Donegal tweed)

164 yds (150 m) per 3.5-oz (100-g) ball

Find this yarn on crochet.com or visit yarnsub.com to find comparable substitutes.

Yardage:
6 (7, 8, 9, 10) (11, 13, 14, 15) balls or 950 (1025, 1250, 1450, 1500) (1800, 2075, 2225, 2400) yds [869 (938, 1143, 1326, 1372) (1646, 1898, 2035, 2195) m]

Note: Budget friendly!

Substitute WeCrochet City Tweed Aran with any similar aran or heavy worsted weight, category #4 yarn that matches gauge. Some lighter-weight category #5 yarns may work well with this pattern, too—just be sure to check your gauge before beginning.

Main gauge hook:
Size U.S. J/10 (6 mm) or size needed to obtain gauge

Hook for collar ribbing:
Size U.S. I/9 (5.5 mm) or hook that is 0.5–1 mm smaller than main gauge hook (this hook is for the collar ribbing only—it is your preference how tight you would like it to be

Notions:
Tapestry needle, six locking stitch markers

Note on stitch markers: You will need a total of six markers: four markers to mark each of the four corner yoke increases and two additional markers to mark the short rows.

Gauge:
4 x 4" (10 x 10 cm) = 11.5 sts x 11 rows in stitch pattern with main gauge (larger) hook (see instructions below)

Ch 16.

Row 1: Sc in 2nd ch from hook, *dc in next ch, sc in next ch; rep from * to end of row, turn. [15 sts]

Row 2: Ch 1, Sc in first sc, *dc in next dc, sc in next sc; rep from * to end of row, turn.

Rep Row 2 until work measures 6 inches (15 cm).

Block your swatch. Measure the inner 4 inches (10 cm) of your blocked swatch to get the most accurate measurement.

ABBREVIATIONS
Written in U.S. crochet terms
ch: chain
ch-sp: chain space
cont: continue
dc: double crochet
FDC: foundation double crochet (see
Foundation Stitches in the Techniques
section on page 176)
FSC: foundation single crochet (see
Foundation Stitches in the Techniques
section on page 172)
PM: place marker
rep: repeat
rnd(s): round(s)
sc: single crochet
scBLO: single crochet in the back loop only
sk: skip
sl st: slip stitch
st(s): stitch(es)
tch: turning chain
work in patt: work in pattern (sc in each sc
and dc in each dc)

Schematic

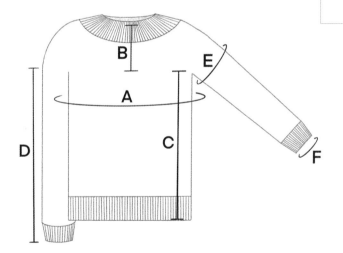

Whispering Pines Sizing Chart

	A FINISHED BUST CIRCUMFERENCE	B YOKE DEPTH MEASURED FROM FINISHED NECKLINE EDGE TO LAST YOKE ROW	C BODY LENGTH MEASURED FROM UNDERARM	D SLEEVE LENGTH MEASURED FROM UNDERARM	E UPPER ARM CIRCUMFERENCE	F WRIST CIRCUMFERENCE
XS	32" 81 cm	8" 20 cm	13.75" 35 cm	20.25" 51.5 cm	12.5" 32 cm	8" 20 cm
S	34.75" 88 cm	9.25" 23 cm	13.75" 35 cm	20.25" 51.5 cm	14" 36 cm	8.5" 22 cm
M	39" 99 cm	9.75" 25 cm	13.75" 35 cm	20" 51 cm	14.5" 37 cm	8.5" 22 cm
L	44.5" 113 cm	10.5" 27 cm	13.75" 35 cm	19" 48 cm	16" 41 cm	9" 23 cm
XL	47.25" 120 cm	10" 25 cm	13.75" 35 cm	19" 48 cm	16.75" 43 cm	9" 23 cm
2X	52.75" 134 cm	10.75" 27 cm	13.75" 35 cm	18.75" 47.5 cm	18.75" 48 cm	9.5" 24 cm
3X	55.25" 140 cm	10.75" 27 cm	13.75" 35 cm	18.75" 47.5 cm	20" 51 cm	9.5" 24 cm
4X	59.75" 152 cm	11" 28 cm	13.75" 35 cm	18.5" 47 cm	24.25" 62 cm	9.5" 24 cm
5X	62.5" 159 cm	12.5" 32 cm	13.75" 35 cm	17.25" 44 cm	25" 64 cm	9.5" 24 cm

This chart shows the finished garment measurements. This sweater is designed to be worn with up to 2 inches (5 cm) of positive ease. When choosing a size, find the bust measurement in this chart that is closest to 2 inches (5 cm) larger than your actual bust measurement depending on your desired amount of positive ease and make this size. For reference, the model is 5 feet, 4 inches (163 cm) tall with a 34-inch (86-cm) bust and is wearing a size small with a finished garment bust measurement of 34.75 inches (88 cm), worn with 0.75 inches (2 cm) of positive ease. If between sizes, size down.

For more information and tester photos, visit knitsnknots.ca/whispering-pines.

Whispering Pines Pattern

Yoke

Use a U.S. J/10 (6 mm) crochet hook or main gauge (larger) hook.

Rnd 1: [FSC 1, FDC 1] 7 (7, 7, 8, 8) (8, 8, 8, 8) times, PM in last dc, [FSC 1, FDC 1] 6 times, PM in last dc, [FSC 1, FDC 1] 14 (14, 14, 16, 16) (16, 16, 16, 16) times, PM in last dc, [FSC 1, FDC 1] 6 times, PM in last dc, [FSC 1, FDC 1] 7 (7, 7, 8, 8) (8, 8, 8, 8) times, sl st into first FSC to join rnd, turn. [80 (80, 80, 88, 88) (88, 88, 88, 88) sts]

Yoke Section 1: Rapid Increases

XS and S: Sk Rnd 2, proceed to Rnd 3.

Move each marker to new st denoted with * (applies to the following rnd only).

Rnd 2 (M–5X only): [Work in patt to marked dc, (dc, sc, dc*) in this dc, cont in patt to next marked dc, (dc*, sc, dc) in marked dc] 2 times, work in patt to end of rnd, sl st to join, turn. [x (x, 88, 96, 96) (96, 96, 96, 96) sts]

XL, 2X, 3X: Rep Rnd 2. [x (x, x, x, 104) (104, 104, x, x) sts]

All Sizes

For the remainder of the yoke, move each marker up to the new ch-1 sp with each subsequent rnd.

Rnd 3: Ch 1, [work in patt to marked dc, (dc, ch 1, dc) in marked dc] 4 times, sc in next sc, cont in patt to end of rnd, sl st into first dc to join, turn. [88 (88, 96, 104, 112) (112, 112, 104, 104) sts]

Rnd 4: *Work in patt to ch-sp, (sc, ch 1, sc) in ch-sp; rep from * 3 more times, work in patt to end of rnd, sl st to join, turn. [96 (96, 104, 112, 120) (120, 120, 112, 112) sts]

Rnd 5: *Work in patt to ch-sp, (dc, ch 1, dc) in ch-sp; rep from * 3 more times, work in patt to end of rnd, sl st to join, turn. [104 (104, 112, 120, 128) (128, 128, 120, 120) sts]

Rep the last 2 rnds x (x, x, 1, 2,) (3, 5, 8, 8) more times.

Stitch Count Checkpoint: 104 (104, 112, 136, 160) (176, 208, 248, 248) sts (including the four corner chains)

Total Rnds Worked: 4 (4, 5, 7, 10) (12, 16, 21, 21)

4X: Skip Yoke Section 2; Proceed to Short Rows

Yoke Section 2: Slower Increase Rate

This section is a 4-rnd repeat. Round count will start at 1 for simplicity.

Move marker directly up to new corner stitch; sometimes this will be a ch, sometimes a sc or dc.

Rnd 1: *Work in patt to ch-sp, sc in ch-sp; rep from * 3 more times, work in patt to end of rnd, sl st to join, turn.

Rnd 2: *Work in patt to marked sc, (sc, ch 1, sc) in marked sc; rep from * 3 more times, work in patt to end of rnd, sl st to join, turn. [112 (112, 120, 144, 168) (184, 216, x, 256) sts]

Rnd 3: *Work in patt to ch-sp, dc in ch-sp; rep from * 3 more times, work in patt to end of rnd, sl st to join, turn.

Rnd 4: *Work in patt to marked dc, (dc, ch 1, dc) in marked dc; rep from * 3 more times, work in patt to end of rnd, sl st to join, turn. [120 (120, 128, 152, 176) (192, 224, x, 264) sts]

Rep the last four rnds 1 (2, 2, 2, 1) (1, x, x, x) more times.

Stitch Count Checkpoint: 136 (152, 160, 184, 192) (208, 224, 248, 264) sts

Total Rnds Worked: 12 (16, 17, 19, 18) (20, 20, 21, 25)

Short Rows

The edge with the seam is the **back** of your sweater. Cut the working yarn and weave in the end. Flip your work so that the V's of the stitches are facing away from you in order to keep the back-and-forth rows consistent.

You are going to join yarn to the back corner of your yoke to work 4 back-and-forth rows along the back edge only. This will raise the back-neck and allow for a better-fitting sweater.

Row 1: Join new yarn with a sl st at the corner ch-sp on the right-hand side along the back-edge of your yoke (see **Figure 1 and Figure 2**), ch 1, dc in first dc, *sc in next sc, dc in next dc; rep from * to next ch-sp, turn. [41 (45, 49, 57, 61) (65, 69, 73, 77) sts]

Figure 1: New yarn has been attached to the corner ch-sp.

Figure 2: Close-up of first dc worked.

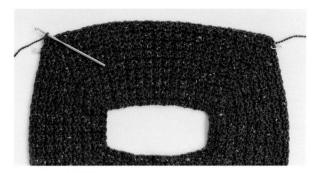

Figure 3: Row 1 has been completed. Next, you will turn your work to begin crocheting Row 2.

Rows 2–4: Ch 1, work in patt to end of row, turn.

Fasten off and weave in ends.

Place a distinct marker in the first and last st of Row 4 to denote the last short row. You will need to refer to these marked sts when working the body.

Note: You should now have 6 stitch markers placed in your yoke: 4 from the corners of your yoke and 2 from the short rows.

Separating Body & Sleeves

Next, you will rejoin the yarn in the center-back.

Find the approximate center sc st on the back edge of your yoke (the same edge as your short rows) and attach yarn into this sc with a sl st.

Note: This sl st must be joined into a sc, not a dc.

Next Rnd: Ch 1, sc in same sc as sl st, work in patt to end of row (the first corner), ch 5 (5, 7, 7, 7) (11, 11, 13, 13), sk entire sleeve edge and second ch-sp, dc in first dc on front edge of sweater, cont in patt to third ch-sp, sk ch-sp, ch 5 (5, 7, 7, 7) (11, 11, 13, 13), sk entire sleeve edge, dc in first dc on back edge, cont in patt to end of rnd (your last st should be a dc), sl st into first sc to join rnd, turn. [92 (100, 112, 128, 136) (152, 160, 172, 180) sts]

Remove the markers from the corners of your yoke and place them into the first and last st of each skipped sleeve edge (four markers total) to help identify the first and last sleeve st—you will need to refer to these markers when you work the first sleeve round.

Body

Rnd 1: Ch 1, dc in first dc, *sc in next sc, dc in next dc; rep from * to underarm chs, sc in first ch, [dc in next ch, sc in next ch] 2 (2, 3, 3, 3) (5, 5, 6, 6) times, cont in patt to next underarm chs, sc in first ch, [dc in next ch, sc in next ch] 2 (2, 3, 3, 3) (5, 5, 6, 6) times, cont in patt to end of rnd, join with sl st, turn.

Work in patt for 28 more rnds or until 3.5 inches (9 cm) shorter than your desired length.

Do not fasten off, continue with working yarn to Bottom Hem Ribbing.

Bottom Hem Ribbing

Continue with the same yarn from Body and a U.S. J/10 (6 mm) crochet hook or main gauge (larger) hook.

Ch 15.

Row 1: Sc in 2nd ch from hook and in each ch across. [14 sc]

Find the st along the last rnd from the body that your first ribbing ch came out of. Do not work into this body st, but sl st into the next 2 sts of the body. Turn work to begin working back on this row just completed.

Row 2: [No tch] Sk the 2 sl st just made, scBLO in each sc to last sc, sc in last sc, turn.

Row 3: [No tch] Sc in first sc, scBLO in each remaining sc to end of row, sl st into next 2 body sts, turn.

Rep Rows 2 and 3 until you have worked your way around your entire sweater. Fasten off, leaving a 10-inch (25-cm) tail to seam the first and last row of ribbing together with a tapestry needle using the whip stitch (see Techniques on page 167) or seaming method of your choice. Weave in ends.

Neckline Ribbing

This ribbing is done the same way as the bottom hem ribbing.

Customization Tip: For a wider head opening, opt for a shorter, more subtle border by working a shorter beginning chain, then following the remaining instructions as written.

Using U.S. I/9 (5.5 mm) crochet hook or smaller hook, join yarn to neckline at the center of the back-neck with a sl st.

Ch 11.

Row 1: Sc in 2nd ch from hook and in each ch across, sl st in next 2 yoke sts, turn. [10 sc]

Row 2: [No tch] Sk the 2 sl st just made, scBLO in each sc to last sc, sc in last sc, turn.

Row 3: [No tch] Sc in first sc, scBLO into each remaining sc to end of row, sl st into next 2 yoke sts, turn.

Rep Rows 2 and 3 until you have worked around the entire neckline.

Fasten off, leaving a 10-inch (25-cm) tail to seam the first and last row of ribbing together with a tapestry needle using the whip stitch or seaming method of your choice. Weave in ends.

Sleeves

Because you added short rows to the back, your right and left sleeves will have one minor difference when working the very first round.

Using U.S. J/10 (6 mm) crochet hook or main gauge (larger) hook, join new yarn with a sl st at the approximate center of the underarm. Make sure you are working in the correct direction: The V's of the stitches along the sleeve opening you are working on should be facing the inside of your sweater. (If they are facing you, turn your work inside out OR simply insert your hook through the stitch from the opposite direction.)

When you insert your hook to begin your round in the approximate center of the underarm, the short rows will appear on the **left** (or at the beginning of the round) when working the **right sleeve**, and on the **right** (or at the end of the round) when working the **left sleeve**.

Once you have determined which side is the right and which side is the left, you can remove the distinct marker or scrap yarn you had in your last short row. These were just to help you determine which sleeve is left and which sleeve is right. Each sleeve opening should now have 2 markers denoting the first and last sleeve stitch from when you finished the yoke.

Follow the Round 1 instructions for each sleeve. After Round 1, the sleeve instructions are identical for both sleeves.

"Work X sts evenly before first marker" simply means that there may not be clear places to work the sts, so just work X number of sts as evenly spaced as you can before the marker.

Rnd 1—Right Sleeve
Short rows appear on the left (beginning of rnd)
Follow your size:

XS (S, XL, 4X, 5X): Work the following sts evenly spaced before first marker: sc, [dc, sc] 3 (3, 4, 5, 5) times; you have now reached the first sleeve st from the yoke, dc in marked dc, cont in patt to next marker and dc in this marked dc, cont in patt to work 4 (4, 6, 8, 8) sts evenly spaced to end of rnd, join with sl st, turn. [36 (40, 48, 70, 72) sts]

M (L, 2X, 3X): Work the following sts evenly spaced before first marker: [dc, sc] 4 (4, 5, 5) times; you have now reached the first sleeve st from the yoke, dc in marked dc, cont in patt to next marker, cont in patt to work 5 (5, 7, 7) sts evenly spaced to end of rnd, join with sl st, turn. [42 (46, 54, 58) sts]

Rnd 1—Left Sleeve
Short rows appear on the right (end of rnd)
Follow your size:

XS (S, XL, 4X, 5X): Work the following sts evenly spaced before first marker: [dc, sc] 2 (2, 3, 4, 4) times; you have now reached the first sleeve st from the yoke, dc in marked dc, cont in patt to next marker and dc in this marked dc, cont in patt to work 7 (7, 9, 11, 11) sts evenly spaced to end of rnd, join with sl st, turn. [36 (40, 48, 70, 72) sts]

M (L, 2X, 3X): Work the following sts evenly spaced before first marker: sc [dc, sc] 2 (2, 3, 3) times; you have now reached the first sleeve st from the yoke, dc in marked dc, cont in patt to next marker, cont in patt to work 8 (8, 10, 10) sts evenly spaced to end of rnd, join with sl st, turn. [42 (46, 54, 58) sts]

For the remainder of the sleeve, work the rnds as specified for your size below:
When instructed to decrease, work the rnd as follows: Ch 1, sk first st, work in patt to last st, sk last st, sl st into first st to join rnd, turn. [Decreases rnd by 2 sts]

All non-decrease rnds are worked as follows: Ch 1, work in patt to end of rnd, sl st into first st to join rnd, turn.

Follow your size only; total number of rows given includes the first row just completed.

Size XS: Work in patt until you have completed a total of 46 rnds, decreasing in the following rnds: 15, 30. [32 sts]

Size S: Work in patt until you have completed a total of 46 rnds, decreasing in the following rnds: 10, 20, 30. [34 sts]

Size M: Work in patt until you have completed a total of 45 rnds, decreasing in the following rnds: 10, 20, 30, 40. [34 sts]

Size L: Work in patt until you have completed a total of 43 rnds, decreasing in the following rnds: 8, 16, 24, 32, 40. [36 sts]

Size XL: Work in patt until you have completed a total of 43 rnds, decreasing in the following rnds: 6, 12, 18, 24, 30, 36. [36 sts]

Size 2X: Work in patt until you have completed a total of 42 rnds, decreasing in the following rnds: 5, 10, 15, 20, 25, 30, 35, 40. [38 sts]

Size 3X: Work in patt until you have completed a total of 42 rnds, decreasing in the following rnds: 4, 8, 12, 16, 20, 24, 28, 32, 36, 40. [38 sts]

Size 4X: Work in patt until you have completed a total of 41 rnds, decreasing in the following rnds: 2, 5, 7, 10, 12, 15, 17, 20, 22, 25, 27, 30, 32, 35, 37, 40. [38 sts]

Size 5X: Work in patt until you have completed a total of 38 rnds, decreasing in the following rnds: 4, 6, 8, 10, 12, 14, 16, 18, 20, 22, 24, 26, 28, 30, 32, 34, 36. [38 sts]

Sleeve Cuff Ribbing
This ribbing is done the same way as the bottom hem ribbing and the collar ribbing. Use a U.S. I/9 (5.5 mm) crochet hook or smaller hook.

Ch 11.

Row 1: Sc in 2nd ch from hook and in each ch across. [10 sc]

Find the st that the initial ch came out of. Do not work into this st, but sl st into the next 2 sts from your last sleeve rnd. Turn work to begin crocheting back on this row just completed.

Row 2: [No tch] Sk the 2 sl st just made, scBLO in each sc to last sc, sc in last sc, turn.

Row 3: [No tch] Sc in first sc, scBLO in each remaining sc to end of row, sl st into next 2 sleeve sts, turn.

Rep Rows 2 and 3 until you have worked your way around your entire sleeve. Fasten off, leaving a 10-inch (25-cm) tail to seam the first and last row of ribbing together with a tapestry needle using the whip stitch or seaming method of your choice. Weave in ends.

Rep all instructions for the second sleeve. Block your sweater to the dimensions listed in the Sizing Chart (page 83).

Dressed to Impress

In Your Holiday Best

Special occasions deserve special outfits. Whether you're headed to a work party, attending a family dinner or celebrating New Year's Eve, this chapter consists of eye-catching pieces you'll be excited to show off. With a variety of designs ranging from formal to playful, you'll be able to accommodate any party theme.

These holiday-inspired designs are subtle enough to be worn any other day of the year because it's not the color that makes them holiday-themed, but the formality of the fits and silhouettes. I wanted to design sweaters that could give you the most use, avoiding pieces you'd only pull out of your closet once a year. To get more wear out of your sweater, steer clear of typical holiday colors and choose something you'd love to wear year-round.

This season, don't buy a new outfit. Make a new outfit.

Silent Night
Velvet Cardigan

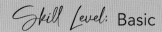
Who wouldn't want to drape themselves in velvet? Whether you're opening presents around the tree or waiting for the ball to drop to begin the new year, this piece is ready for any celebration that comes your way. I'm a big fan of yarn with unexpected textures, and the Silent Night Velvet Cardigan brings a fresh look to crochet with this dazzling sea of velvet stitches. To compensate for the heaviness of the velvet yarn, this pattern is designed with an airy stitch pattern and short sleeves. The weight of this yarn combined with the vertical ribbing and side slits creates an elegant drape and allows for incredible movement during wear. This cardigan is a must-make for anyone who loves to look put-together with minimal effort.

Construction

This oversized cardigan is worked in two identical panels that get partially seamed together along the center-back and along the sides. The two identical body panels are worked side-to-side to create the vertical ribbing that you see running down the length of the cardigan. Two identical short sleeves are worked separately as rectangles that get seamed onto the body.

Materials

Yarn:
Bulky—Bernat Velvet in Blackbird (100% polyester) 315 yds (288 m) per 10.5-oz (300-g) skein

Find this yarn on yarnspirations.com or visit yarnsub.com to find comparable substitutes.

Yardage:
3 (4, 4, 4, 5) skeins or 900 (1000, 1125, 1250, 1350) yds [823 (915, 1029, 1143, 1235) m]

Note: Budget friendly!

Substitute Bernat Velvet with any similar bulky weight, category #5 yarn that matches gauge. For a similar look to the sample shown, choose a polyester yarn with a similar velvety, chenille feel. Non-velvet yarns will work too!

ABBREVIATIONS
Written in U.S. crochet terms
ch: chain
FSC: foundation single crochet (see Foundation Stitches in the Techniques section on page 172)
rep: repeat
sc: single crochet
scBLO: single crochet in the back loop only
st(s): stitch(es)

Hook:
Size U.S. K/10½ (6.5 mm) or size needed to obtain gauge

Notions:
Tapestry needle, several locking stitch markers

Gauge:
4 x 4" (10 x 10 cm) = 14 sts and 10 rows in single crochet through the back loops only

If you are struggling to match gauge, choose the hook that gives you the closest **stitch** gauge. This determines the length of your cardigan and cannot be adjusted once you've started crocheting.

Schematic

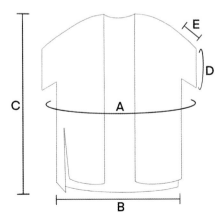

Silent Night Sizing Chart

	A FINISHED BUST CIRCUMFERENCE (INCLUDING FRONT GAP)	B BACK PANEL WIDTH	C TOTAL LENGTH MEASURED FROM TOPS OF SHOULDERS	D SLEEVE CIRCUMFERENCE	E SLEEVE LENGTH
XS	52" 132 cm	26" 66 cm	29.5" 75 cm	21" 53 cm	4" 10 cm
S/M	58" 147 cm	29" 74 cm	29.5" 75 cm	22" 56 cm	4" 10 cm
L/XL	64" 162 cm	32" 81 cm	29.5" 75 cm	22" 56 cm	4" 10 cm
2X/3X	70" 178 cm	35" 89 cm	29.5" 75 cm	23" 58 cm	4" 10 cm
4X/5X	76" 193 cm	38" 97 cm	29.5" 75 cm	23" 58 cm	4" 10 cm

This chart shows the finished garment measurements. This cardigan is designed to be oversized, worn with approximately 14 to 26 inches (36 to 66 cm) of positive ease depending on the size you choose. When choosing a size, find the bust measurement in this chart that equals approximately 14 to 26 inches (33 to 66 cm) larger than your actual bust measurement and make this size. For reference, the model is 5 feet, 4 inches (163 cm) tall with a 34-inch (86-cm) bust and is wearing a size S/M with a finished garment bust measurement of 58 inches (147 cm) with 24 inches (61 cm) of positive ease. If between sizes, size down. For more information and tester photos, visit knitsnknots.ca/silent-night.

Silent Night Pattern

Body Panel (Make 2)

Row 1: FSC 206.

Row 2: Ch 1, sc in first st, scBLO across to last st, sc in last st, turn. [206 sts]

Rep Row 2 until you have a total of 28 (32, 36, 40, 43) rows completed or until your work measures 11.25 (12.75, 14.5, 16, 17.25)" (29 [32, 37, 41, 44] cm).

Customization Tip: For a longer (or shorter) cardigan, add (or subtract) stitches from your beginning foundation chain in multiples of two. The total number of multiples of two you end up adding or subtracting is how many stitches you will add or subtract from the Back Neck Shaping instructions. For example, if you add 10 stitches to your foundation chain, you will add 5 stitches to your first Back Neck Shaping row, finishing with a total of 112 stitches after completing this row.

Note: Work the first and last single crochet of each row a little bit tighter than your regular gauge to keep the bottom edges of your cardigan neat and to prevent them from flaring, especially if you are using a velvet yarn.

Row 29 (33, 37, 41, 44): Ch 1, sc in first st, scBLO in next 105 sts, sc in next st, turn. [107 sts]

Next 3 Rows: Ch 1, sc in first st, scBLO in each st to last st, sc in last st, turn.

Fasten off, leaving a 40-inch (102-cm) tail for seaming the panels (only 1 panel needs a long tail).

Attaching Panels

You currently have two identical panels that each have one wide section. The two wide sections will be seamed together to become the back of your cardigan, and the other half will fold over to become the front panel. To seam together, lay each panel flat with the long, flat edges on the outside and the rows from the Back Neck Shaping touching, mirroring each other. With a tapestry needle, use the long tail you left to seam the Back Neck rows together using the whip stitch (see Techniques on page 167) or seaming method of your choice. Weave in this end. At this point, your work should resemble a U-shape with one large back panel and two symmetrical front panels outstretched.

High-Low Side Split

Next, count 15 stitches up from each of the back-panel corners and mark this stitch. Fold your front panels over so that the front outer corner lines up with this marked stitch, and use locking stitch markers to hold these stitches together before you begin seaming. From here, line up the sides stitch-for-stitch as best you can and use locking stitch markers to help hold them in place. Measure 10 inches (25 cm) from the bottom edge of your front panel and begin seaming at this point to create the side split. For a more dramatic side split, begin seaming at your desired height. With a separate length of yarn (measuring approximately twice the length that you need to seam) and a tapestry needle, seam upward, stopping at about 14 inches (36 cm) from the top shoulder, leaving this space unworked so you can attach the sleeve here later. Do not weave in your tail yet; you will use this to close any gaps after the sleeve is attached.

Sleeves (Make 2)

Row 1: FSC 14, leaving a 16-inch (41-cm) tail for seaming the sleeve closed.

Customization Tip: For a shorter (or longer) sleeve, work fewer (or additional) FSC.

Row 2: [No tch] Sc in first st, scBLO in each st to last st, sc in last st, turn. [14 sts]

Rep Row 2 until you have a total of 52 (55, 55, 58, 58) rows or until work measures 21 (22, 22, 23, 23)" (53 [56, 56, 58, 58] cm).

Customization Tip: The sleeve is meant to be dramatically oversized. For tighter sleeves, work fewer rows than instructed.

Fasten off, leaving a 30-inch (76-cm) tail for seaming the sleeve to your cardigan.

With a tapestry needle and the shorter tail, seam the first and last row of the sleeve together using the whip stitch or seaming method of your choice.

Place the finished sleeve at the arm hole opening on the body with the seam facing down toward the armpit and pin in place using locking stitch markers. Stretch the sleeve an additional inch or two (2.5 to 5 cm) over the body fabric. This allows for better drape in the sleeve. With a tapestry needle, use the long tail remaining from the sleeve to loosely seam the sleeve onto the body of your cardigan. Do not pull tight, otherwise, your sleeve will feel restricting and may pucker. Use any remaining tails to close any gaps. Weave in any remaining ends.

This type of material does not usually require blocking, but feel free to block if desired. Blocking your work will help relax the stitches and improve the drape, especially if you used a non-velvet yarn.

December Romance
Sweater Dress

Introducing my favorite piece in the entire collection and the quintessential holiday dress: December Romance. This versatile dress is sophisticated enough for all of your holiday festivities but subtle and understated enough to wear any day of the year. We skipped the obvious holiday themes—no red, green or sparkles on this one!—and what remains is a sexy, tasteful sweater dress suitable to rock year-round.

This striking design artfully accentuates the feminine figure with optional waist shaping. Enjoy the romantic, billowy collar and off-the-shoulder fit, perfectly juxtaposed against the figure-hugging silhouette of this body. Casual elements like the oversized collar and relaxed sleeves make this dress more suitable for everyday wear. Whether you're celebrating the new year as the clock strikes midnight or in need of a new party outfit, this dress is sure to make you feel beautiful, no matter your personal style.

Construction

This sweater has a circular yoke construction, worked seamlessly from the top down. After completing the yoke increases, the yoke is then separated to create space for the body and the armholes. The body is worked next with some optional waist shaping and then the sleeves. Last, the billowy, ribbed collar is added.

Materials

Yarn:
Worsted—Lion Brand Jeans in Stovepipe (100% acrylic) 246 yds (225 m) per 3.5-oz (100-g) skein

Find this yarn on lionbrand.com or visit yarnsub.com to find comparable substitutes.

Skill Level: Easy

Yardage:
8 (9, 10, 11, 11) (13, 14, 14, 15) skeins or 1950 (2025, 2225, 2500, 2650) (3000, 3225, 3425, 3600) yds [1784 (1852, 2035, 2286, 2424) (2744, 2949, 3132, 3292) m]

Note: Budget friendly!

Substitute Lion Brand Jeans with any similar worsted weight, category #4 yarn that matches gauge. Any fiber should work out fine. Choose something soft (key: not itchy) that you would want to wear against your skin for long periods of time. I chose Jeans specifically for this fitted dress because this yarn has a softness that is hard to find in acrylics within this price range.

Yarn Note: This design is comprised of single crochet stitches throughout, encouraging you to get creative with your yarn choices. Simple stitches like this are great opportunities to use any special, unique yarns you may have on hand that you want to show off without getting lost in a distracting stitch pattern. Speckled, variegated, self-striping, and hand-dyed yarns pair best with a blank canvas of simple stitches to really let the yarn shine.

Main gauge hook:
Size U.S. G/7 (4.5 mm) or size needed to obtain gauge

Hook for fold-over collar only:
Size U.S. I/9 (5.5 mm) or size needed to obtain gauge for collar

Notions:
Tapestry needle, six locking stitch markers

Main Gauge:
5 x 5" (13 x 13 cm) = 22 sts and 24 rows in single crochet worked in the round with main gauge (smaller) hook

(continued)

Collar gauge:
4 x 4" (10 x 10 cm) = 14.5 sts and 12 rows in single crochet worked in the back loops only, measured unstretched. These 12 rows should be able to stretch to 7 inches (18 cm). The collar is crocheted loosely; you may need to go up a hook size if you are typically a tight crocheter. It is better to err on the looser side than the tighter side for this collar. Additional information regarding the collar can be found in the Collar section of the pattern (page 103).

Note: The right side is the side that faces you as you are crocheting the yoke, body and sleeves.

Sweater Version: To make a sweater that lands at the hips, work the pattern as written and simply stop at your desired length. You may choose to omit the waist and hip shaping for a more relaxed fit.

Schematic

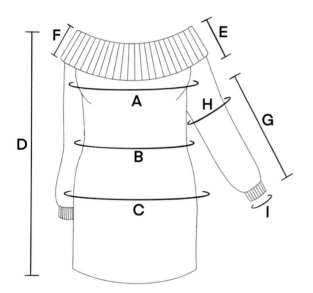

ABBREVIATIONS
Written in U.S. crochet terms
BOR: beginning of round
ch: chain
inc: increase—work 2 single crochets into designated stitch
PM: place marker
rep: repeat
rnd: round
sc: single crochet
sc2tog: single crochet 2 stitches together
scBLO: single crochet in the back loop only
sk: skip
sl st: slip stitch
st(s): stitch(es)

December Romance Sizing Chart

	A FINISHED BUST CIRCUM-FERENCE	B WAIST CIRCUM-FERENCE	C HIPS CIRCUM-FERENCE	D TOTAL LENGTH MEASURED FROM FIRST YOKE ROW TO BOTTOM OF DRESS	E YOKE DEPTH MEASURED FROM FIRST YOKE ROUND TO LAST YOKE ROUND	F COLLAR HEIGHT	G SLEEVE LENGTH MEASURED FROM UN-DERARM	H UPPER ARM CIRCUM-FERENCE	I WRIST CIRCUM-FERENCE
XS	30" 76 cm	23" 58 cm	32" 81 cm	29.5" 75 cm	3.5" 9 cm	10.5" 27 cm	19.75" 50 cm	10.5" 27 cm	8" 20 cm
S	34" 86 cm	27" 69 cm	36.5" 93 cm	30" 76 cm	3.75" 9.5 cm	11" 28 cm	19.5" 49.5 cm	11.5" 29 cm	8" 20 cm
M	38" 97 cm	31" 79 cm	40" 102 cm	31" 79 cm	4" 10 cm	11" 28 cm	19.25" 49 cm	12" 30 cm	8" 20 cm
L	42" 107 cm	35" 89 cm	44.5" 113 cm	33.5" 85 cm	4" 10 cm	11" 28 cm	19" 48 cm	13" 33 cm	8" 20 cm
XL	46" 117 cm	39" 99 cm	48" 122 cm	34.5" 88 cm	4.5" 11 cm	11.5" 29 cm	18.75" 47.5 cm	14.25" 36 cm	8" 20 cm
2X	50" 127 cm	43" 109 cm	52" 132 cm	36" 91 cm	4.5" 11 cm	11.5" 29 cm	18.75" 47.5 cm	16.75" 43 cm	9" 23 cm
3X	54" 137 cm	47" 119 cm	56.5" 144 cm	36" 91 cm	4.75" 12 cm	11.5" 29 cm	18.5" 47 cm	18" 46 cm	9" 23 cm
4X	58" 147 cm	51" 130 cm	62" 157 cm	36" 91 cm	5" 12.5 cm	12" 30 cm	18.25" 46.5 cm	19.5" 50 cm	9" 23 cm
5X	62" 157 cm	55" 140 cm	64.5" 164 cm	36.5" 93 cm	5.25" 13 cm	12" 30 cm	18" 46 cm	19.5" 50 cm	9" 23 cm

This chart shows the finished garment measurements. This sweater dress is designed to be worn with approximately 0 to 2 inches (0 to 5 cm) of positive ease. Find the finished bust measurement in this chart and choose a size that is 0 to 2 inches (0 to 5 cm) larger than your actual bust measurement. For reference, the model is 5 feet, 4 inches (163 cm) tall with a 34-inch (86-cm) bust and is wearing a size small with a finished garment bust measurement of 34 inches (86 cm) with 0 inches (0 cm) of positive ease. If between sizes, size down.

For more information and tester photos, visit knitsnknots.ca/december-romance.

December Romance Pattern

Yoke

Use a size U.S. G/7 (4.5 mm) crochet hook or smaller gauge hook.

Ch 105 (105, 105, 108, 111) (111, 111, 114, 114). Sc into first ch to join rnd and set yourself up to work in a spiral. Place BOR marker.

Rnd 1: Sc in each ch to end of rnd. [105 (105, 105, 108, 111) (111, 111, 114, 114) sc]

Increase Rnd 1

*Inc in next st, sc in next 2 sts; rep from * to end of rnd. [140 (140, 140, 144, 148) (148, 148, 152, 152) sc]

Sc in each st for next 4 (4, 3, 3, 4) (3, 3, 2, 2) rnds.

Increase Rnd 2

*Inc in next st, sc in next 3 sts; rep from * to end of rnd. [175 (175, 175, 180, 185) (185, 185, 190, 190) sc]

Sc in each st for next 4 (4, 3, 3, 4) (3, 3, 3, 3) rnds.

Increase Rnd 3

XS: Sc in first 5 sts, *inc in next st, sc in next 9 sts; rep from * to end of rnd. [192 sc]

All remaining sizes: *Inc in next st, sc in next 4 sts; rep from * to end of rnd. [x (210, 210, 216, 222) (222, 222, 228, 228) sc]

Sc in each st for next 5 (6, 3, 3, 4) (3, 3, 2, 2) rnds.

Sizes XS and S finished with yoke; skip to Separating Body & Sleeves. All remaining sizes continue to Increase Rnd 4.

Increase Rnd 4

M: Sc in first st, *inc in next st, sc in next 18 sts; rep from * to end of rnd. [221 sc]

L: Sc in first 9 sts, *inc in next st, sc in next 8 sts; rep from * to end of rnd. [239 sc]

XL: Sc in first 12 sts, *inc in next st, sc in next 4 sts; rep from * to end of rnd. [264 sc]

All remaining sizes: *Inc in next st, sc in next 5 sts; rep from * to end of rnd. [x (x, x, x, x) (259, 259, 266, 266) sc]

Sc in each st for next x (x, 5, 6, 4) (3, 3, 3, 3) rnds.

Sizes M, L, and XL finished with yoke; skip to Separating Body & Sleeves. All remaining sizes continue to Increase Rnd 5.

Increase Rnd 5

All remaining sizes: *Inc in next st, sc in next 6 sts; rep from * to end of rnd. [x (x, x, x, x) (296, 296, 304, 304) sc]

Sc in each st for next x (x, x, x, x) (4, 3, 2, 2) rnds.

Size 2X finished with yoke; skip to Separating Body & Sleeves. All remaining sizes continue to Increase Rnd 6.

Increase Rnd 6

3X: Sc in first 8 sts, *inc in next st, sc in next 11 sts; rep from * to end of rnd. [320 sc]

All remaining sizes: *Inc in next st, sc in next 7 sts; rep from * to end of rnd. [x (x, x, x, x) (x, x, 342, 342) sc]

Sc in each st for next x (x, x, x, x) (x, 1, 3, 3) rnds.

Size 3X finished with yoke; skip to Separating Body & Sleeves. All remaining sizes continue to Increase Rnd 7.

4X: Sc in first 2 sts, *inc in next st, sc in next 67 sts; rep from * to end of rnd. [347 sc]

5X: Sc in first 12 sts, *inc in next st, sc in next 21 sts; rep from * to end of rnd. [357 sc]

Sc in each st for next x (x, x, x, x) (x, x, 1, 2) rnds.

At this point, your yoke should now have a total of 17 (18, 19, 20, 21) (22, 23, 24, 25) rnds completed.

Separating Body & Sleeves

Make sure your BOR marker is centered.

Sc in next 29 (32, 35, 39, 42) (46, 50, 54, 57) sts, ch 8 (10, 13, 15, 16) (18, 19, 20, 22), sk next 38 (40, 40, 42, 47) (56, 60, 66, 64) sts to create space for right sleeve, sc in next 58 (65, 70, 77, 85) (92, 100, 107, 114) sts, ch 8 (10, 13, 15, 16) (18, 19, 20, 22), sk next 38 (40, 40, 42, 47) (56, 60, 66, 64) sts to create space for left sleeve, sc in next 29 (33, 36, 39, 43) (46, 50, 54, 58) sts to BOR. [132 (150, 167, 185, 202) (220, 238, 255, 273) sts]

PM in first and last skipped st of each sleeve (2 markers per sleeve). You will use these markers when working the first round of your sleeves.

Body

Next Rnd: Sc in each sc and each ch to end of rnd.

Sc in each st around until sweater reaches the bottom of your bust to begin the waist shaping. If omitting waist shaping, continue to sc in each st until desired length, then proceed to Finishing Row.

Waist Shaping

Make sure BOR marker is in the center-back of your sweater. If it has drifted off-center, simply replace it into the center now.

Note: Refer to the waist measurements given for your size in the Sizing Chart (page 99). If you think this measurement needs to be adjusted to fit your waist, you can add more space by simply working fewer decrease rnds—or fewer decreases within those rnds—as you see fit. Alternatively, if you would like the waist of your dress to be tighter than the number provided in the Sizing Chart, work additional decrease rnds until achieving your desired fit. Focus more on the fit rather than following these numbers to a tee. Feel free to use these decrease rnds as a guideline—the most important thing is that you are happy with the way the dress is fitting your unique body measurements.

Decrease Rnd 1: Starting at BOR marker at back of sweater, sc in first 29 (32, 35, 38, 42) (46, 50, 53, 57) sts, PM in this last st to mark where your waist shaping will begin (you will be working decreases across the front of your sweater only), *sc in next 6 (7, 8, 9, 10) (11, 12, 13, 14) sts, sc2tog; rep from * 9 more times, sc in each st to BOR. [122 (140, 157, 175, 192) (210, 228, 245, 263) sc]

Sc in each st for next 4 rnds.

Decrease Rnd 2: Sc in each st up to and including first marked st, *sc in next 5 (6, 7, 8, 9) (10, 11, 12, 13) sts, sc2tog; rep from * 9 more times, sc in each st to BOR. [112 (130, 147, 165, 182) (200, 218, 235, 253) sc]

Sc in each st for next 4 rnds.

Decrease Rnd 3: Sc in each st up to and including first marked st, *sc in next 4 (5, 6, 7, 8) (9, 10, 11, 12) sts, sc2tog; rep from * 9 more times, sc in each st to BOR. [102 (120, 137, 155, 172) (190, 208, 225, 243) sc]

Sc in each st until sweater reaches the top of your hips where you will begin increasing to make space for the hips. This shaping will be evenly spaced around the entire dress, so you can now remove the st marker from the decreasing section.

Customization Tip: Refer to the hip measurements given for your size in the Sizing Chart (page 99). If you think this measurement needs to be adjusted to fit your hips, you can add more space by simply working additional increase rnds—or additional increases within those rnds—as you see fit. Alternatively, if you would like your dress to fit tighter in the hips, work fewer increase rnds—or fewer increases within those rnds—until achieving your desired fit. Focus more on the fit rather than following these numbers to a tee. Feel free to use these increase rnds as a guideline—the most important thing is that you are happy with the way the dress is fitting your unique body measurements.

Increase Rnd 1: Sc in first 2 (0, 7, 5, 2) (0, 8, 5, 3) sts, *sc in next 9 (11, 12, 14, 16) (18, 19, 21, 23) sts, inc in next st; rep from * to BOR. [112 (130, 147, 165, 182) (200, 218, 235, 253) sc]

Sc in each st for next 4 rnds.

Increase Rnd 2: Sc in first 2 (0, 7, 5, 2) (0, 8, 5, 3) sts, *sc in next 10 (12, 13, 15, 17) (19, 20, 22, 24) sts, inc in next st; rep from * to BOR. [122 (140, 157, 175, 192) (210, 228, 245, 263) sc]

Sc in each st for next 4 rnds.

Increase Rnd 3: Sc in first 2 (0, 7, 5, 2) (0, 8, 5, 3) sts, *sc in next 11 (13, 14, 16, 18) (20, 21, 23, 25) sts, inc in next st; rep from * to BOR. [132 (150, 167, 185, 202) (220, 238, 255, 273) sc]

Sc in each st for next 4 rnds.

Increase Rnd 4: Sc in first 2 (0, 7, 5, 2) (0, 8, 5, 3) sts, *sc in next 12 (14, 15, 17, 19) (21, 22, 24, 26) sts, inc in next st; rep from * to BOR. [142 (160, 177, 195, 212) (230, 248, 265, 283) sc]

Shaping is complete.

Sc in each st around until body measures 26 (26.5, 27, 29, 30) (31, 31, 31, 31)" (66 [67, 69, 74, 76] [79, 79, 79, 79] cm) or until desired length.

Finishing row: Once satisfied with length, sl st into next st, ch 1, turn to begin working in the opposite direction, sc in next st, PM in this st to mark first st of rnd, sc in each st around until reaching marked st, sl st into marked st, fasten off, weave in ends.

Sleeves

Attach yarn with sl st into approximate center of underarm with the right side facing you.

Work 4 (5, 6, 7, 8) (9, 9, 10, 11) sc evenly before first marker, sc in next 38 (40, 40, 42, 47) (56, 60, 66, 64) sleeve sts up to and including second marked st, work 4 (5, 7, 8, 8) (9, 10, 10, 11) sc evenly to end of rnd, work 1 sc directly into first sc to begin working in a spiral. [46 (50, 53, 57, 63) (74, 79, 86, 86) sc]

Sc in each st around until you have worked a total of 82 (81, 49, 19, 13) (20, 26, 11, 10) rows.

XS and S: Skip to Wrist.

All remaining sizes:

Decrease rnd: Sc2tog, sc in each st around. [Decreases rnd by 1 st]

Next x (x, 9, 9, 4) (2, 1, 1, 1) row(s): Sc in each st around.

Rep from Decrease rnd x (x, 2, 5, 12) (18, 24, 31, 31) more times. [x (x, 50, 51, 50) (55, 54, 54, 54) sc]

Wrist

Next rnd: Sc all sts while working 10 decreases evenly throughout rnd. [36 (40, 40, 41, 40) (45, 44, 44, 44) sc]

Next rnd: Sc all sts while working 1 (5, 5, 6, 5) (5, 4, 4, 4) decreases evenly throughout rnd. [35 (35, 35, 35, 35) (40, 40, 40, 40) sc]

Next rnd: Sc in each st around.

At this point, your sleeve should now have a total of 85 (84, 82, 82, 81) (80, 79, 78, 77) rnds completed.

Cuff

Ch 11.

Row 1: Sc in 2nd ch from hook and in each ch across, sl st into next 2 sleeve sts, turn.

Row 2: Skip the 2 sl st just made, scBLO in each st across until 1 st remains, sc in last st, turn.

Row 3: Ch 1, sc in first st, scBLO in each st to end of row, sl st into next 2 sleeve sts, turn.

Rep Rows 2–3 until you have worked your way back to starting point. Fasten off, leaving a tail for seaming the cuff. Use your tapestry needle to stitch your first and last rows together using the slip stitch or any seaming method of your choice. Weave in ends.

Rep all instructions for the second sleeve.

Collar

The collar is worked on a larger hook. The sample shown is crocheted with a loose tension using a U.S. I/9 (5.5 mm) hook, but you can play around with a few different hook sizes and use the one that produces your desired fabric. This ribbing should be loose with dramatically more stretch than the body of your sweater because it must fold over and stretch across your shoulders and chest. You want this to have a relaxed fit without feeling tight or restricting. If you are debating between which hook to use, err on the larger side. If you typically have a tight tension, you may want to use a U.S. K/10½ (6.5 mm) hook.

Try to keep a loose tension for the entirety of the collar.

Row 1: Working back on the ch, sc into 2nd ch from hook and in each ch across, sl st into next 2 sts along neckline, turn. [38 (40, 40, 40, 42) (42, 42, 44, 44) sc]

Row 2: Skip 2 sl st just made, scBLO in each st across until 1 st remains, sc in last st, turn.

Row 3: Ch 1, sc in first st, scBLO in each st to end of row, sl st into next 2 sts along neckline, turn.

Rep Rows 2–3 until you have worked your way across the entire neckline.

Customization Tip: If you are partway through your collar and worry it may be too tight, you can make a small change to your Row 3 reps by working a sl st into just 1 st along the neckline instead of working a sl st into the next 2 sts along the neckline. Work this modification as many times as you see fit; this will allow room for additional rows of ribbing without requiring you to rip back and restart your collar with a looser tension.

Once you have worked your way around the entire neckline, fasten off, leaving a long tail for seaming the first and last rows together. Use a tapestry needle to seam the first and last rows together using the whip stitch (see Techniques on page 167) or any seaming method of your choice.

Weave in any remaining ends and block the dress to the dimensions listed in the Sizing Chart (page 99).

Customization Tip: For a shorter (or longer) fold-over collar, work fewer (or additional) chains than instructed.

Use a U.S. I/9 (5.5 mm) hook, or larger gauge hook.

Attach yarn with a sl st to the neckline at the center-back of the sweater, ch 39 (41, 41, 41, 43) (43, 43, 45, 45).

Sugarplum
Off-the-Shoulder Yoke

This wintry, off-the-shoulder piece is simple in construction, but majestic and stately in appearance. This design explores the juxtaposition of a chunky, winter yarn with a seemingly lightweight design. The neat, uniform stitches create a smooth, continuous fabric that lies effortlessly on your body like a freshly fallen blanket of snow. The inherent bulkiness of the yarn combined with a tight stitch pattern creates a structured, rigid fabric. Rather than trying to resist this, I played it to my advantage and used it as a design feature—an opportunity to create an oversized, boxy statement piece that accentuates the stiffness and structure of the garment.

This easy-to-crochet sweater can easily be worked up in any size within just a few days—perfect for those who are new to garment-making.

Note: Once you've mastered this pattern, you may want to try the Amber Magic Off-the-Shoulder Yoke (page 151)—a flowy, fingering weight version of this sweater with a little more shaping in the arms.

Construction

This sweater has a circular yoke construction, worked seamlessly from the top down. After completing the yoke increases, the yoke is then separated to create space for the body and the armholes. The body is worked next, and the sleeves are worked last.

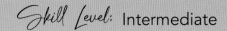

Skill Level: Intermediate

Materials

Yarn:
Bulky—WeCrochet Biggo in Bare (50% superwash Merino wool, 50% nylon)

110 yds (100 m) per 3.5-oz (100-g) hank

Find this yarn on crochet.com or visit yarnsub.com to find comparable substitutes.

Yardage:
7 (7, 8, 9, 10) (11, 12, 14, 14) hanks or 700 (750, 850, 975, 1050) (1200, 1300, 1450, 1525) yds [641 (686, 778, 892, 961) (1098, 1189, 1326, 1395) m]

Note on Yardage: Yardage is for a slightly cropped sweater and three-quarters-length sleeves as shown in the sample and the Sizing Chart (page 107). Additional yardage will be needed if you would like a full-length sweater or longer sleeves.

Note: Biggo is listed as a bulky weight, category #5 yarn and leans toward the lighter side of this category. Despite this, the fabric in the sweater shown is quite dense when paired with the chosen stitch pattern. For best results, choose a worsted weight or aran weight, category #4 yarn for a less dense fabric that will provide better drape than a bulky weight as long as gauge is matched. If you choose to use bulky weight yarn as I did in the sample shown, I recommend you choose a breathable fiber like wool and avoid non-breathable fibers like acrylic if possible. Make sure to swatch your chosen yarn to be sure you are satisfied with the resulting fabric before continuing.

Hook:
Size U.S. K/10½ (6.5 mm) or size needed to obtain gauge

Notions:
Tapestry needle, five locking stitch markers

Gauge:
3 x 3″ (8 x 8 cm) = 6.5 sts and 10 rows in center single crochet worked in the round

Schematic

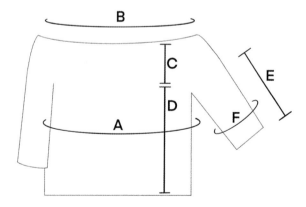

ABBREVIATIONS
Written in U.S. crochet terms

BOR: beginning of round
ch: chain
csc: center single crochet (see Techniques on page 179)
inc: increase—work 2 csc into designated stitch
PM: place marker
rep: repeat
rnd: round
sc: single crochet
sk: skip
sl st: slip stitch
st(s): stitch(es)

Sugarplum Sizing Chart

	A FINISHED BUST CIRCUMFERENCE	B NECK OPENING CIRCUMFERENCE	C YOKE DEPTH MEASURED FROM FIRST YOKE ROUND TO LAST YOKE ROUND	D BODY LENGTH MEASURED FROM UNDERARM	E SLEEVE LENGTH MEASURED FROM UNDERARM	F UPPER ARM CIRCUMFERENCE
XS	33" 84 cm	32" 81 cm	5.5" 14 cm	9" 23 cm	9.5" 24 cm	13.5" 34 cm
S	37" 94 cm	33" 84 cm	6" 15 cm	9.5" 24 cm	9.5" 24 cm	13.75" 35 cm
M	41" 104 cm	33" 84 cm	6" 15 cm	10" 25 cm	9.5" 24 cm	14.75" 37 cm
L	45" 114 cm	33" 84 cm	6.25" 16 cm	10.5" 27 cm	9.5" 24 cm	15.75" 40 cm
XL	49" 124 cm	33" 84 cm	6.25" 16 cm	11" 28 cm	9.5" 24 cm	17" 43 cm
2X	53" 135 cm	33" 84 cm	6.5" 17 cm	11.5" 29 cm	9.5" 24 cm	19" 48 cm
3X	57" 145 cm	34.5" 88 cm	7" 18 cm	12" 30 cm	9.5" 24 cm	20.25" 51 cm
4X	61" 155 cm	34.5" 88 cm	7.25" 18.5 cm	12.5" 32 cm	9.5" 24 cm	22" 56 cm
5X	65" 165 cm	34.5" 88 cm	7.25" 18.5 cm	13" 33 cm	9.5" 24 cm	22" 56 cm

This chart shows the finished garment measurements. This sweater is designed to be worn with approximately 3 to 5 inches (8 to 13 cm) of positive ease. Find the finished bust measurement in this chart and choose a size that is 3 to 5 inches (8 to 13 cm) larger than your actual bust measurement. For reference, the model is 5 feet, 4 inches (163 cm) tall with a 34-inch (86-cm) bust and is wearing a size small with a finished garment bust measurement of 37 inches (94 cm) with 3 inches (8 cm) of positive ease. If between sizes, size down.

For more information and tester photos, visit knitsnknots.ca/sugarplum.

Sugarplum Pattern

Pattern Notes

Right Side: The "right side" is the side of your work that faces you as you are crocheting it.

Yoke

Ch 69 (72, 72, 72, 72) (72, 75, 75, 75), sl st into first ch to join rnd, turn.

Rnd 1: Sc loosely in each ch to end of row. (The next rnd will be difficult to work if Rnd 1 is too tight!) [69 (72, 72, 72, 72) (72, 75, 75, 75) sc]

Work 1 csc straight into the first sc from Rnd 1 to set yourself up to work in a spiral. Place BOR marker into this csc.

Rnd 2: Csc in each sc to end of rnd.

Notes: Because you are working in a spiral, your BOR marker will gradually drift off-center. Simply replace it into the approximate center st as often as needed, using the tail from the beginning chain as a reference point.

In the first few rounds it may be more difficult to find the proper stitch placement. Once you have a few rounds worked, you will find your rhythm and it will become much easier!

Increase Rnd 1

All Sizes: *Inc in next st, csc in next 2 sts; rep from * to end of rnd. [92 (96, 96, 96, 96) (96, 100, 100, 100) csc]

XS only—next rnd: Csc all sts while working 2 increases evenly spaced to bring st count to 94 csc.

All sizes: Csc in each st for next 14 (2, 2, 2, 2) (2, 2, 2, 2) rnds.

Size XS finished with yoke; skip to Separating Body & Sleeves. All other sizes continue to Increase Rnd 2.

Customization Tip: Refer to the yoke depth measurement in the Sizing Chart (page 107). You may want to try your sweater on periodically to see where the finished yoke would lie on your body. If it seems too deep for you, you can eliminate non-increase rnds before separating the yoke as you see fit.

Increase Rnd 2

S: *Inc in next st, csc in next 11 sts; rep from * to end of rnd. [104 csc]

M: *Inc in next st, csc in next 5 sts; rep from * to end of rnd. [112 csc]

L, XL, 2X, 3X, 4X and 5X: *Inc in next st, sc in next 3 sts; rep from * to end of rnd. [x (x, x, 120, 120) (120, 125, 125, 125) csc]

Csc in each st for next x (14, 2, 2, 2) (2, 2, 2, 2) rnds.

Size S finished with yoke; skip to Separating Body & Sleeves. All other sizes continue to Increase Rnd 3.

Increase Rnd 3

M: Csc in first 2 sts, *inc in next st, csc in next 21 sts; rep from * to end of rnd. [117 csc]

L: *Inc in next st, csc in next 11 sts; rep from * to end of rnd. [130 csc]

XL: *Inc in next st, csc in next 5 sts; rep from * to end of rnd. [140 csc]

2X, 3X, 4X and 5X: *Inc in next st, csc in next 4 sts; rep from * to end of rnd. [x (x, x, x, x) (144, 150, 150, 150) csc]

Csc in each st for next x (x, 11, 12, 12) (2, 2, 2, 2) rnds.

Sizes M, L and XL finished with yoke; skip to Separating Body & Sleeves. All other sizes continue to Increase Rnd 4.

Increase Rnd 4

2X: *Inc in first st, csc in next 10 sts; rep from * to last st, csc in last st. [157 csc]

3X: Csc in first 10 sts, *inc in next st, csc in next 9 sts; rep from * to end of rnd. [164 csc]

4X: Csc in first 10 sts, *csc in next 4 sts, inc in next st; rep from * to last 10 sts, csc in last 10 sts. [176 csc]

5X: *Inc in next st, csc in next 5 sts; rep from * to end of rnd. [175 csc]

Csc in each st for next x (x, x, x, x) (10, 11, 12, 2) rnds.

Sizes 2X, 3X and 4X finished with yoke; skip to Separating Body & Sleeves. Size 5X continue to Increase Rnd 5.

Increase Rnd 5

5X: Csc in first 5 sts, *inc in next st, csc in next 16 sts; rep from * to end of row. [185 csc]

5X only: Csc in each st for next 9 rnds.

Size 5X finished with yoke; proceed to Separating Body & Sleeves.

All sizes: At this point, your yoke should now have a total of 18 (20, 20, 21, 21) (22, 23, 24, 24) rnds completed.

Separating Body & Sleeves
Make sure your BOR marker is centered.

Csc in next 14 (16, 18, 21, 22) (25, 26, 27, 29) sts, ch 8 (8, 8, 8, 9) (9, 11, 12, 12), sk next 19 (20, 22, 24, 26) (30, 31, 34, 34) sts to create space for right sleeve, csc in next 28 (32, 37, 41, 44) (48, 51, 54, 59) sts, ch 8 (8, 8, 8, 9) (9, 11, 12, 12), sk next 19 (20, 22, 24, 26) (30, 31, 34, 34) sts to create space for left sleeve, csc in next 14 (16, 18, 20, 22) (24, 25, 27, 29) sts to BOR. [72 (80, 89, 98, 106) (115, 124, 132, 141) sts]

PM in first and last skipped st of each sleeve (2 markers per sleeve). You will need to refer to these markers when working the first sleeve round.

Body

BOR marker can now be removed.

All Sizes: Csc in each csc and each ch to end of rnd.

Csc in each st around until body measures 9 inches (23 cm) from underarm or until desired length. When satisfied with length, sl st into next 3 sts and fasten off.

> *Note:* This stitch pattern creates a dense fabric without much stretch. Adding length to your sweater may make it feel restricting and challenging to take on and off. Try it on as you crochet it to make sure you like the way it feels before adding more length.

Sleeves

Attach yarn with sl st into approximate center of underarm with the right side facing you.

Rnd 1 (Set-Up Rnd): Work 5 (5, 5, 5, 5) (5, 6, 7, 7) csc evenly before first marker, csc in next 19 (20, 22, 24, 26) (30, 31, 34, 34) sleeve sts up to and including second marked st, work 5 (5, 5, 5, 6) (6, 7, 7, 7) csc evenly to end of rnd. [29 (30, 32, 34, 37) (41, 44, 48, 48) csc]

Csc directly into first csc from Set-Up Rnd to begin working in a spiral, then csc in each st around until sleeve measures 9.5 inches (24 cm) or until desired length. When satisfied with length, sl st into next 3 sts and fasten off.

> *Customization Tip:* The sleeves of this sweater are designed to be roomy and shapeless, without any decreasing. If you would like more tapered sleeves, you can decrease as often as you like by working 2 sts together, but keep these decreases in line with the center-underarm (where you attached your yarn to begin the sleeves) so that the decreases are less visible. Keep in mind that this yarn and stitch pattern is not very stretchy, so you will not want to make your sleeves too tight.

Rep all instructions for the second sleeve. Weave in any remaining ends and block your sweater to the dimensions listed in the Sizing Chart (page 107).

Champagne Glow
Single-Sleeve Sweater

No collection of sweaters would be complete without including at least one unconventional silhouette. From the asymmetrical neckline to the delicate, single sleeve, this unique sweater packs a punch. The eye is drawn to the delicate sleeve that blooms into the generously wide wrist, adding a dynamic, playful element. The gracefully asymmetrical neckline is comfortable to wear and stays in place thanks to the snug fit and the placement of the single shoulder. The neckline and sleeve are a dynamic duo, coming together to form a striking holiday sweater or a flirty top for your next night out.

Construction

The body of this sweater is worked in two identical pieces that get seamed together while leaving an armhole opening for the sleeve to be worked directly onto the edge of the opening. The sleeve is worked flat without any shaping until increasing at the wrist to create the wide, scalloped silhouette. It is then seamed lengthwise when completed.

Materials

Yarn:
Sport—Debbie Bliss Baby Cashmerino in Mustard (55% wool, 33% acrylic, 12% cashmere)

137 yds (125 m) per 1.8-oz (50-g) skein

Find this yarn on lovecrafts.com or visit yarnsub.com to find comparable substitutes.

Skill Level: Easy

Yardage:
9 (10, 10, 12, 13) (15, 16, 18, 19) skeins or 1175 (1250, 1350, 1550, 1750) (1950, 2150, 2450, 2575) yds [1074 (1143, 1234, 1417, 1600) (1782, 1965, 2240, 2354) m]

Note: Budget-friendly alternatives include Lion Brand LB Collection Superwash Merino, Premier Cotton Fair, Premier Anti-Pilling Everyday DK Merino Blend, WeCrochet Brava Sport, WeCrochet Wool of the Andes Sport.

Substitute Debbie Bliss Baby Cashmerino with any similar sport weight, category #2 yarn that matches gauge. Choose a fiber with some bounce and avoid fibers that will grow substantially after blocking or washing. It is important that your sweater lies snug to your body because too much growth will cause the sweater to sag.

Hook:
Size U.S. F/5 (3.75 mm) crochet hook or size needed to obtain gauge

Notions:
Tapestry needle, interlocking stitch markers

Gauge:
5.5 x 5.5" (14 x 14 cm) = 5 shells and 18 rows in shell stitch (see instructions below)

Row 1: FSC 43.

Row 2–4: Follow instructions for Body Panel Rows 2–4.

Rep Rows 3 and 4 until your swatch measures approximately 7 inches (18 cm) in height.

Block your swatch. Measure the inner 5.5 inches (14 cm) of your blocked swatch to get the most accurate measurement.

ABBREVIATIONS
Written in U.S. crochet terms
ch: chain
dc: double crochet
FSC: foundation single crochet (see Foundation Stitches in the Techniques section on page 172)
hdc: half double crochet
rep: repeat
sc: single crochet
shell: work 5 dc into designated stitch
sk: skip
sl st: slip stitch
st(s): stitch(es)
tch: turning chain

Schematic

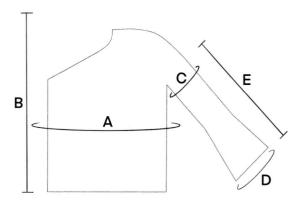

Champagne Glow Sizing Chart

	A	B	C	D	E
	FINISHED BUST CIRCUMFERENCE	TOTAL LENGTH MEASURED FROM TOP OF SHOULDER	UPPER ARM CIRCUMFERENCE	WRIST CIRCUMFERENCE	SLEEVE LENGTH MEASURED FROM UNDERARM
XS	28.5" 72 cm	18.5" 47 cm	10" 25 cm	12.5" 32 cm	19" 48 cm
S	33" 84 cm	19.25" 49 cm	11" 28 cm	14" 36 cm	17.75" 45 cm
M	37.5" 95 cm	20" 51 cm	11" 28 cm	14" 36 cm	16.5" 42 cm
L	42" 107 cm	21" 53 cm	12" 30 cm	15.5" 39 cm	15.5" 39 cm
XL	46" 117 cm	21.75" 55 cm	14.5" 37 cm	14" 36 cm	14.5" 37 cm
2X	48.5" 123 cm	23" 58 cm	15.5" 39 cm	15.5" 39 cm	15.5" 39 cm
3X	53" 135 cm	23.5" 60 cm	17.5" 44 cm	18.25" 46 cm	14.75" 37 cm
4X	57" 145 cm	25.25" 64 cm	18.75" 48 cm	19.5" 50 cm	13.75" 35 cm
5X	61.5" 156 cm	26" 66 cm	18.75" 48 cm	19.5" 50 cm	12.5" 32 cm

This chart shows the finished garment measurements. This sweater looks best when fitted and is designed to be worn with approximately 1 inch (2.5 cm) of negative ease to 1 inch (2.5 cm) of positive ease but should not be worn with any more than 1 inch (2.5 cm) of positive ease. Find the finished bust measurement in this chart and choose a size that is within +/– 1 inch (2.5 cm) of your actual bust measurement or go down a full size or even two for additional negative ease. For reference, the model is 5 feet, 4 inches (163 cm) tall with a 34-inch (86-cm) bust and is wearing a size small with a finished garment bust measurement of 33 inches (84 cm) with approximately 1 inch (2.5 cm) of negative ease. If between sizes, size down.

For more information and tester photos, visit knitsnknots.ca/champagne-glow.

Champagne Glow Pattern

Body Panel (Make 2)

Row 1: Leaving a 24-inch (61-cm) tail for seaming the sides of your sweater, FSC 79 (91, 103, 115, 127) (133, 145, 157, 169).

Row 2: Ch 1, sc in first st, *sk next 2 sts, shell in next st, sk next 2 sts, sc in next st; rep from * to end of row, turn. [13 (15, 17, 19, 21) (22, 24, 26, 28) shells]

Row 3: Ch 2, 3 dc in first sc, *sk next 2 dc, sc in next dc, sk next 2 dc, shell in next sc; rep from * to end of row, omitting the shell of your very last rep, work 3 dc in final sc of row, turn.

Row 4: Ch 1, sc in first dc, *sk next 2 dc, shell in next sc, sk next 2 dc, sc in next dc; rep from * to end of row, turn.

Rep Rows 3–4 until you have worked a total of 46 (46, 46, 48, 48) (52, 52, 56, 56) rows. If you matched gauge, this should be approximately 14 (14, 14, 14.75, 14.75) (16, 16, 17, 17)" (36 [36, 36, 37, 37] [41, 41, 43, 43] cm). This is the length of the body of your sweater up to your underarm before the asymmetrical neckline shaping begins.

Customization Tip: If you would like your sweater to be longer or shorter than written for your size, add or subtract rows in multiples of 2 as you see fit. You should finish on a Row 4 rep. Make note of how many rows you added or eliminated so that you can make the same alteration to both panels.

Asymmetrical Neckline Shaping

Each row decreases by half a shell.

Row 1: Ch 2, 3 dc in first sc, *sk 2 dc, sc in next dc, sk next 2 dc, shell in next sc; rep from * across, stopping once you have worked a shell in between the last and next-to-last shell in the row below, sk next 2 dc, sl st into next dc, turn. [12.5 (14.5, 16.5, 18.5, 20.5) (21.5, 23.5, 25.5, 27.5) shells]

Row 2: [No tch] Sl st into next 2 dc, sc in next dc, *sk next 2 dc, shell in next sc, sk next 2 dc, sc in next dc; rep from * to end of row, turn. [12 (14, 16, 18, 20) (21, 23, 25, 27) shells]

Rep Rows 1 and 2 until you have completed a total of 15 (17, 19, 21, 23) (23, 25, 27, 29) decreasing rows, ending on a Row 1 rep. [5.5 (6.5, 7.5, 8.5, 9.5) (10.5, 11.5, 12.5, 13.5) shells]

Next, you will work a finishing row to even out the undulating shell stitches and get a top edge that is flat and uniform for easier seaming.

Finishing Row: Ch 2, dc in first sl st, *hdc in next dc, sc in next dc, sl st in next dc, sc in next dc, hdc in next dc, dc in next sc; rep from * 4 (5, 6, 7, 8) (9, 10, 11, 12) more times, hdc in next st, sc in next st, sl st in last st, cut yarn, leaving a tail for seaming.

Assembly

Lay your two panels over one another in the same orientation. With a tapestry needle, seam along the tops of the shoulder edges using the whip stitch (see Techniques on page 167) or seaming method of your choice. Align the sides stitch-for-stitch as evenly as you can with locking stitch markers, starting from the bottom and working your way up. Seam the longer side (sleeve side) with the 24-inch (61-cm) tail from one of your Body panels using the whip stitch or seaming method of your choice, leaving an opening measuring 5 (5.5, 5.5, 6, 7.25) (8, 8.75, 9.5, 9.5)" (13 [14, 14, 15, 18] [20, 22, 24, 24] cm) from the tops of the shoulders to create room for the sleeve. Seam the shorter side all the way to the top (with a separate length of yarn measuring at least 24 inches [61 cm]) using the whip stitch or seaming method of your choice and fasten off.

Sleeve

Attach yarn with a sl st at the bottom of the sleeve opening (the armpit) to begin working the first sleeve row. First sc will be placed in same place as sl st.

The first row of the sleeve is worked directly onto the body by crocheting as evenly as possible into the edge of the sleeve opening. There are no clear stitches to work into as there normally are when crocheting; this is more intuitive. Place your stitches so that they are as evenly spaced as you can, with similar spacing to what you have been doing so far. You can use the top shoulder seam as a halfway point to help with spacing.

Row 1: Ch 1, sc in this same space, [work 1 shell, work 1 sc] a total of 9 (10, 10, 11, 13) (14, 16, 17, 17) times around your sleeve opening until reaching the beginning of your row on the opposite side. Turn work to begin working in the opposite direction; you will seam the sleeve closed at the end. [9 (10, 10, 11, 13) (14, 16, 17, 17) shells]

Row 2: Ch 2, 3 dc in first sc, *sk next 2 dc, sc in next dc, sk next 2 dc, shell in next sc; rep from * to end of row, omitting the shell of your very last rep, work 3 dc in final sc of row, turn.

Row 3: Ch 1, sc in first dc, *sk next 2 dc, shell in next sc, sk next 2 dc, sc in next dc; rep from * to end of row, turn.

Sizes XS, S, M and L skip to "All Sizes" on page 118.

XL (2X, 3X, 4X, 5X) only
Row 4: Ch 2, sc into center dc of first shell, *sk next 2 dc, shell in next sc, sk next 2 dc, sc in next dc; rep from * until you have worked into the final complete shell of the row below, sk next 2 dc, dc into final sc of row, turn. [12 (13, 15, 16, 16) shells]

Row 5: Ch 2, sk first dc, 3 dc in first sc, sk next 2 dc, sc in next dc, sk next 2 dc, *shell in next sc, sk next 2 dc, sc in next dc, sk next 2 dc; rep from * across until you have worked a sc into the final complete shell of the row below, sk next 2 dc, 3 dc in last sc, turn.

Row 6: Rep Row 3.

Row 7: Rep Row 2.

Row 8: Rep Row 3.

Rep Rows 2–8 two more times.

You should now have 10 (11, 13, 14, 14) shells.

Next Row: Ch 2, 4 dc in first sc, *sk next 2 dc, sc in next dc, sk next 2 dc, shell in next sc; rep from * to end of row, omitting last shell, work 4 dc in final sc of row, turn.

Next Row: Ch 1, sc in first dc, *sk next 3 dc, shell in next sc, sk next 3 dc, sc in next dc; rep from * to end of row, turn.

Rep last 2 rows for an additional 5.5 inches (14 cm) or until sleeve reaches the desired length. Fasten off, leaving a 24-inch (61-cm) tail for seaming. With a tapestry needle, use this tail to seam the length of your sleeve closed using the whip stitch or seaming method of your choice. Once you reach the underarm, seam any remaining gap that may be left at the underarm. Weave in all ends and block your sweater to the dimensions listed in the Sizing Chart (page 115). Blocking will improve the drape and flatten out any puckering from your sleeve increases.

Optional Neckline Finishing Row

(Sample shown does not have this finishing row.) If you would like to add a finishing row to the neckline, you can attach yarn to the side seam on the sleeveless part of your sweater and sc evenly around the entire neckline as many times as you like. You may do so in joined, turned rounds or work seamlessly in a spiral—the choice is yours. This step can also help provide additional coverage and tighten the neckline if you crocheted too loosely and will prevent your sweater from stretching over time.

All sizes: Rep Rnd 2 and 3 until sleeve measures 5.5 inches (14 cm) shorter than your desired length. Finish on a Row 3 rep.

From this point on, "shell" means to work 7 dc in the designated st rather than 5. This will contribute to the wide, delicate shape of the sleeve.

Burning Embers
V-Neck

A playful twist on a holiday sweater, Burning Embers features a statement bow closure over a modern, peek-a-boo cutout on the lower back. The festive, oversized bow is not only a striking detail, but serves an important function: a way to incorporate simple waist shaping to hug your natural waistline. This cropped sweater is designed to be close fitting, especially at the waist, so that the bow will stay taut against your back.

While the other patterns in this chapter infer a celebratory theme in more ambiguous, subtle ways, this design undeniably captures the essence of the holiday season. This sweater was designed for parties, date night and anything in between. Once the holidays pass, camouflage it seamlessly into your everyday wardrobe by making one in your favorite color and wearing it year-round.

Construction

First, two separate back pieces are worked and then joined to create the back cutout. The rest of the back panel is worked in back-and-forth rows until reaching your desired sweater length. Then, the work splits into two symmetrical sections to create the V-neck, and these two sections are joined at the base of the V-neck to work the rest of the front side of the sweater to the same length as the back panel. The body is folded at the shoulders, and seamed at the sides, leaving space for armholes. The sleeves are worked from the bottom up in joined rounds and then seamed onto the body. The bow is worked last and is sewn across the cutout on the lower back.

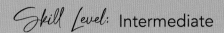

Skill Level: Intermediate

Materials

Yarn:
Worsted—Red Heart Soft in Wine (100% acrylic)
256 yds (234 m) per 5-oz (141-g) skein
Find this yarn on yarnspirations.com or visit yarnsub.com to find comparable substitutes.

Yardage:
4 (4, 4, 5, 5) (5, 6, 6, 6) skeins or 850 (925, 1000, 1075, 1150) (1250, 1325, 1400, 1500) yds [778 (846, 915, 983, 1052) (1143, 1212, 1281, 1372) m]

Note on Yardage: Different colorways of Red Heart Soft have varying yardage. Make sure to check the yardage listed on the label of your desired colorway to ensure you have enough yarn before beginning. Yardage listed here is based on the length provided for your size in the Sizing Chart on page 122. If you would like a longer sweater than written for your size, additional yardage will be required.

Note: Budget friendly!

Substitute Red Heart Soft for any worsted weight, category #4 yarn that matches gauge. Any fiber you choose should produce a beautiful sweater.

Hook:
Size U.S. H/8 (5 mm) or size needed to obtain gauge

Notions:
Tapestry needle, several locking stitch markers

(continued)

Gauge:

4 x 4" (10 x 10 cm) = 16 sts and 16 rows in stitch pattern (see instructions below)

Ch 20.

Row 1: Sc in 2nd ch from hook, *ch 1, sk next ch, sc in next ch; rep from * to end of row, turn. [10 sc; 9 ch-sp]

Row 2: Ch 1, sc in first sc, *ch 1, sk next ch-sp, sc in next sc; rep from * to end of row, turn.

Rep Row 2 until you have at least 18 rows worked.

Block your swatch. Measure the inner 4 inches (10 cm) of your blocked swatch to get the most accurate measurement. Within these 4 inches (10 cm), you should have 8 sc and 8 ch, or 16 stitches total.

Schematic

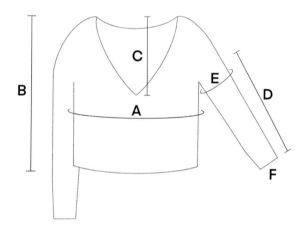

Stitch Pattern: This stitch pattern uses alternating single crochets and chains, where you will always sc into each sc, and ch 1 and skip over every ch-sp.

Burning Embers Sizing Chart

	A FINISHED BUST CIRCUMFERENCE	B TOTAL LENGTH MEASURED FROM TOPS OF SHOULDERS	C V-NECK DEPTH MEASURED FROM TOPS OF SHOULDERS	D SLEEVE LENGTH MEASURED FROM UNDERARM	E UPPER ARM CIRCUMFERENCE	F WRIST CIRCUMFERENCE
XS	28.5" 72 cm	16.5" 42 cm	9" 23 cm	20" 51 cm	11.25" 29 cm	7.75" 20 cm
S	32.5" 83 cm	17" 43 cm	9.5" 24 cm	19.5" 50 cm	11.75" 30 cm	8.25" 21 cm
M	36.5" 93 cm	17.25" 44 cm	9.5" 24 cm	18.5" 47 cm	12.25" 31 cm	8.75" 22 cm
L	40.5" 103 cm	17.5" 44 cm	9.5" 24 cm	18" 46 cm	13.25" 34 cm	8.75" 22 cm
XL	44.5" 113 cm	17.75" 45 cm	9.5" 24 cm	17" 43 cm	14.75" 37 cm	8.75" 22 cm
2X	48.5" 123 cm	18" 46 cm	10" 25 cm	16.5" 42 cm	17.25" 44 cm	8.75" 22 cm
3X	52.5" 133 cm	18" 46 cm	10" 25 cm	15.5" 39 cm	18.25" 46 cm	9.25" 23 cm
4X	56.5" 144 cm	18.5" 47 cm	10" 25 cm	15" 38 cm	19.75" 50 cm	9.25" 23 cm
5X	60.5" 154 cm	18.5" 47 cm	10" 25 cm	14.5" 37 cm	19.75" 50 cm	9.75" 25 cm

This chart shows the finished garment measurements. This sweater is designed to be close fitting, worn with 1.5 inches (4 cm) of negative ease to 0.5 inch (1 cm) of positive ease, depending on your actual bust measurement. When choosing a size, find the bust measurement in this chart that is closest to your actual bust measurement and make this size. For reference, the model is 5 feet, 4 inches (163 cm) tall with a 34-inch (86-cm) bust and is wearing a size small with a finished garment bust measurement of 32.5 inches (83 cm), worn with 1.5 inches (4 cm) of negative ease. If between sizes, size down.

For more information and tester photos, visit knitsnknots.ca/burning-embers.

Burning Embers Pattern

To create the peek-a-boo back opening, the back panel begins with two separate sections that will later join to become one piece.

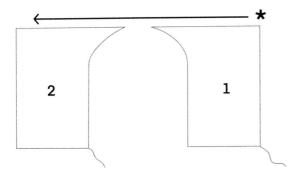

Figure 1: Two symmetrical pieces will be worked, then oriented to have the increases toward the middle. Next, you will work across Side 1, work a specified number of chains, and then work across Side 2 to connect your work.

Back Panel

Side 1

Row 1: FSC 11 (15, 19, 23, 25) (29, 31, 33, 37), turn.

Row 2: Ch 1, sc in first st, *ch 1, sk next st, sc in next st; rep from * to end of row, turn. [6 (8, 10, 12, 13) (15, 16, 17, 19) sc; 5 (7, 9, 11, 12) (14, 15, 16, 18) ch-sp]

Row 3–18: Ch 1, sc in first sc, *ch 1, sk next ch-sp, sc in next sc; rep from * to end of row, turn.

Row 19: Ch 1, sc in first sc, *ch 1, sk next ch-sp, sc in next sc; rep from * until 1 ch-sp and 1 sc remains, ch 1, sc in next ch-sp, ch 1, sc in last sc, turn. [7 (9, 11, 13, 14) (16, 17, 18, 20) sc; 6 (8, 10, 12, 13) (15, 16, 17, 19) ch-sp]

Row 20–21: Rep Row 18–19. [8 (10, 12, 14, 15) (17, 18, 19, 21) sc; 7 (9, 11, 13, 14) (16, 17, 18, 20) ch-sp]

Row 22: Rep Row 18.

You will come back to this piece; do not cut yarn. Pull the loop up and put a stitch marker in your live loop to easily replace your hook back into this stitch later. Proceed to Side 2.

Side 2

Row 1: With new yarn, FSC 11 (15, 19, 23, 25) (29, 31, 33, 37), turn.

Row 2: Ch 1, sc in first st, *ch 1, sk next st, sc in next st; rep from * to end of row, turn. [6 (8, 10, 12, 13) (15, 16, 17, 19) sc; 5 (7, 9, 11, 12) (14, 15, 16, 18) ch-sp]

Row 3–18: Ch 1, sc in first sc, *ch 1, sk next ch-sp, sc in next sc; rep from * to end of row, turn.

Row 19: Ch 1, sc in first sc, ch 1, sc in first ch-sp, ch 1, sc in next sc; *ch 1, sk next ch-sp, sc in next sc; rep from * to end of row, turn. [7 (9, 11, 13, 14) (16, 17, 18, 20) sc; 6 (8, 10, 12, 13) (15, 16, 17, 19) ch-sp]

Row 20–21: Rep Row 18–19. [8 (10, 12, 14, 15) (17, 18, 19, 21) sc; 7 (9, 11, 13, 14) (16, 17, 18, 20) ch-sp]

Row 22: Rep Row 18.

Cut yarn, fasten off.

Joining Row

Return to live loop from Side 1 and insert your hook into the live stitch. Referring to Figure 1, we will begin Row 23 at the upper right-hand corner of Side 1, work across Side 1, increasing in the last st, then work a number of chains specified for your size, work directly into the last st from Side 2, work an increase in the same st, and then work in the established stitch pattern to the end of the row. This will connect both sections and allow you to work back and forth across the entire width for the remainder of the Back Panel until you are ready to split for the V-Neck.

Lay work as shown in Figure 1 with the two increase edges toward the middle, facing each other.

Row 23: Ch 1, sc in first sc, *ch 1, sk next ch-sp, sc in next sc*; rep from * to * across Side 1 until 1 sc and 1 ch-sp remain unworked, ch 1, sc in next ch-sp, ch 1, sc in last sc, ch 23 (23, 23, 23, 27) (27, 31, 35, 35), sc directly into the first sc of Side 2, ch 1, sc in next ch-sp, ch 1, sc in next sc, rep from * to * to end of row, turn. [9 (11, 13, 15, 16) (18, 19, 20, 22) sc and 8 (10, 12, 14, 15) (17, 18, 19, 21) ch-sp on each side of chain; 23 (23, 23, 23, 27) (27, 31, 35, 35) ch in middle]

Row 24: Ch 1, sc in first st, *ch 1, sk next st, sc in next sc; rep from * to end of row, turn. [29 (33, 37, 41, 45) (49, 53, 57, 61) sc; 28 (32, 36, 40, 44) (48, 52, 56, 60) ch-sp]

Rep Row 24 an additional 42 (44, 45, 46, 47) (48, 48, 50, 50) more times, or until work measures 16.5 (17, 17.25, 17.5, 17.75) (18, 18, 18.5, 18.5)" (42 [43, 44, 44, 45] [46, 46, 47, 47] cm) from first row. Do not fasten off, you will continue with the same yarn to work the Front.

Customization Tip: For a shorter (or longer) sweater, work fewer (or additional) repeats here.

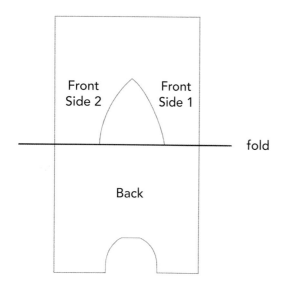

Figure 2: This is what the body of your sweater will look like. You will create a cutout for the V-neck by working Side 1 and Side 2, similar to the back cutout. You will continue to increase toward the center until you are ready to connect your work and finish the remainder of the front of your sweater.

Place a marker on the edges of your last row to mark the tops of the shoulders. Next, you will create the front panel V-neck. Similar to how you began the back panel, the V-neck will be worked in two separate sections and then joined at the base of the V-neck to work the remainder of the front of the sweater as shown in Figure 2.

Front

V-Neck Side 1

(Continuing with same yarn)

Row 1: Ch 1, sc in first sc, *ch 1, sk next ch-sp, sc in next sc; rep from * 7 (8, 10, 12, 14) (15, 17, 19, 21) more times, turn. [9 (10, 12, 14, 16) (17, 19, 21, 23) sc; 8 (9, 11, 13, 15) (16, 18, 20, 22) ch-sp]

Row 2–26: Ch 1, sc in first sc, *ch 1, sk next ch-sp, sc in next sc; rep from * to end of row, turn.

Customization Tip: For a more modest V-neck, work fewer reps than listed above, then follow pattern as written. Make the same adjustment to V-Neck Side 2. After joining your V-neck, work the front length until it matches the length of the back side.

Row 27: Ch 1, sc in first sc, *ch 1, sk next ch-sp, sc in next sc; rep from * until 1 sc and 1 ch-sp remain unworked, ch 1, sc in next ch-sp, ch 1, sc in last sc, turn. [10 (11, 13, 15, 17) (18, 20, 22, 24) sc; 9 (10, 12, 14, 16) (17, 19, 21, 23) ch-sp]

Row 28: Ch 1, sc in first sc, *ch 1, sk next ch-sp, sc in next sc; rep from * to end of row, turn.

Rep last 2 rows 4 (5, 5, 5, 5) (6, 6, 6, 6) more times. [14 (16, 18, 20, 22) (24, 26, 28, 30) sc; 13 (15, 17, 19, 21) (23, 25, 27, 29) ch-sp]

Fasten off.

V-Neck Side 2

Count 9 (10, 12, 14, 16) (17, 19, 21, 23) sc from unworked edge and attach new yarn with sl st into this sc. The first sc of Row 1 will be worked into the same st as this sl st.

Rows 1–26: Ch 1, sc in first sc, *ch 1, sk next ch-sp, sc in next sc; rep from * to end of row, turn. [9 (10, 12, 14, 16) (17, 19, 21, 23) sc; 8 (9, 11, 13, 15) (16, 18, 20, 22) ch-sp]

Row 27: Ch 1, sc in first sc, ch 1, sc in next ch-sp, ch 1, sc in next sc, *ch 1, sk next ch-sp, sc in next sc; rep from * to end of row, turn. [10 (11, 13, 15, 17) (18, 20, 22, 24) sc; 9 (10, 12, 14, 16) (17, 19, 21, 23) ch-sp]

Row 28: Ch 1, sc in first sc, *ch 1, sk next ch-sp, sc in next sc; rep from * to end of row, turn.

Rep last 2 rows 4 (5, 5, 5, 5) (6, 6, 6, 6) more times. [14 (16, 18, 20, 22) (24, 26, 28, 30) sc; 13 (15, 17, 19, 21) (23, 25, 27, 29) ch-sp]

After finishing the last row, do not turn work. You will continue crocheting in this direction to work across V-Neck Side 1 and join your work.

V-Neck Joining Row

Continuing from the end of your last rep of Row 28, ch 3, sc directly into first sc from V-Neck Side 1 to join row, *ch 1, sk next ch-sp, sc in next sc; rep from * to end of row, turn.

Row 29: Ch 1, sc in first sc, *ch 1, sk next ch-sp, sc in next sc; rep from * to end of row, cont in patt across the center ch-3, turn. [29 (33, 37, 41, 45) (49, 53, 57, 61) sc; 28 (32, 36, 40, 44) (48, 52, 56, 60) ch-sp]

Rep last row 30 (30, 31, 32, 33) (32, 32, 34, 34) more times, or until front panel measures 16.5 (17, 17.25, 17.5, 17.75) (18, 18, 18.5, 18.5)" (42 [43, 44, 44, 45] [46, 46, 47, 47] cm) from first V-neck row.

If you adjusted the length on your back panel, make the same adjustment here. Note that if you feel your V-neck is too deep after completing your front panel, you can try working additional rows to your front panel. This will add some length to your sweater but will help to raise your neckline without you having to rip back and redo it.

Fasten off, leaving a 24-inch (61-cm) tail for seaming the sides of your sweater.

Fold your sweater in half along the tops of the shoulders so that your first and last rows match up. Starting from the bottom, seam the sides of your sweater with a tapestry needle using the whip stitch (see Techniques on page 167) or seaming method of your choice. Stop at approximately 6 (6, 7, 7, 8) (9, 10, 10, 10)" (15 [15, 18, 18, 20] [23, 25, 25, 25] cm) from the tops of the shoulders to leave space to attach the sleeves. Do not fasten off yet; you will come back to this side seam after you sew on the sleeves to close any remaining gaps.

Sleeves (Make 2)

Row 1: FSC 31 (33, 35, 35, 35) (35, 37, 37, 39), turn.

Rnd 2: Ch 1, sc in first st, *ch 1, sk next st, sc in next st; rep from * to end of row, sl st into first sc to join in the round, turn. [16 (17, 18, 18, 18) (18, 19, 19, 20) sc; 15 (16, 17, 17, 17) (18, 18, 19) ch-sp]

With a tapestry needle and the tail from your foundation ch, seam Row 1 closed using the whip stitch or seaming method of your choice.

For the remainder of the sleeve, work the rnds as specified for your size below:

When instructed to increase, work the round as follows: Ch 1, sc in first sc, ch 1, sc in first ch-sp, ch 1, sc in next sc, *ch 1, sk next ch-sp, sc in next sc; rep from * to end of rnd, sl st into first sc to join, turn. [Increases rnd by 1 sc and 1 ch]

"Cont in patt": Ch 1, sc in first sc, *ch 1, sk next ch-sp, sc in next sc; rep from * to end of rnd, sl st into first sc to join, turn.

Notes: Total rnds provided includes the first 2 rnds you have already completed.

The sleeves are worked in joined rnds; remember to turn your work after each rnd to begin working in the opposite direction.

XS (S, M): Cont in patt for a total of 80 (78, 74) rnds, increasing in the following rnds: 9, 18, 27, 36, 45, 54, 63. [23 (24, 25) sc; 22 (23, 24) ch-sp]

L: Cont in patt for a total of 72 rnds, increasing in the following rnds: 7, 14, 21, 28, 35, 42, 49, 56, 63. [27 sc; 26 ch-sp]

XL: Cont in patt for a total of 68 rnds, increasing in the following rnds: 5, 10, 15, 20, 25, 30, 35, 40, 45, 50, 55, 60. [30 sc; 29 ch-sp]

2X: Cont in patt for a total of 66 rnds, increasing in the following rnds: 3, 6, 11, 14, 19, 22, 27, 30, 35, 38, 43, 46, 51, 54, 59, 62, 65. [35 sc; 34 ch-sp]

3X: Cont in patt for a total of 62 rnds, increasing in the following rnds: 3, 6, 9, 12, 15, 18, 21, 24, 27, 30, 33, 36, 39, 42, 45, 48, 51, 54. [37 sc; 36 ch-sp]

4X: Cont in patt for a total of 60 rnds, increasing in the following rnds: 3, 4, 7, 8, 11, 14, 17, 20, 23, 26, 29, 32, 35, 38, 41, 44, 47, 50, 53, 56, 59. [40 sc; 39 ch-sp]

5X: Cont in patt for a total of 58 rnds, increasing in the following rnds: 3, 4, 7, 8, 11, 14, 17, 20, 23, 26, 29, 32, 35, 38, 41, 44, 47, 50, 53, 56. [40 sc; 39 ch-sp]

Fasten off, leaving a 24-inch (61-cm) tail for seaming the sleeve to the body.

Attaching Sleeves

Lay work flat. Place the sleeves at the armholes with the seam pointing down toward the armpit and use locking stitch markers to align your sts evenly around the sleeve opening on the body panels. Use the tail end to seam the sleeve in place with a tapestry needle using the seaming method of your choice. When seaming the sleeves onto your sweater, keep this seam loose and do not pull tight in order to maintain some stretch; otherwise, this seam will restrict your arms during wear. Use the tail from side seam to close any remaining gaps. Weave in ends.

Finishing Rows

Attach yarn with a sl st to the neckline near the tops of the shoulders or back neck for an inconspicuous join. Ch 1, sc evenly around the entire neckline until reaching starting point, sl st into first sc to join rnd, fasten off. Work additional rounds for a thicker neckline border if desired.

Attach yarn with a sl st to back of sweater at the bottom inner corner of the back cutout. Ch 1, sc evenly around entire cutout until reaching the opposite bottom corner, fasten off.

Bow

See the photo tutorial on page 180 for help with crocheting the bow.

The bow is made of two separate rectangles: one large rectangle for the main bow piece, and one small rectangle to pinch the center of the bow.

Large Rectangle

Customization Tip: For a wider bow than shown in the sample, add chs until reaching your desired width.

With new yarn, ch 38 (38, 38, 38, 42) (42, 46, 50, 50), leaving a 24-inch (61-cm) tail for seaming.

Row 1: Sc in 2nd ch and each ch across, turn. [37 (37, 37, 37, 41) (41, 45, 49, 49) sc]

Row 2: Ch 1, sc in each sc across, turn.

Rep Row 2 until work measures 10 inches (25 cm).

Fasten off, leaving another 24-inch (61-cm) tail for seaming.

Fold your work in half so that the first and last rows are aligned.

Using the two tail ends, seam the three edges of the bow closed with a tapestry needle so that your rectangle is completely closed. Weave in ends.

Small Rectangle
Ch 5.

Row 1: Sc in 2nd ch from hook and in each ch across, turn. [4 sc]

Row 2–13: Ch 1, sc in each sc across, turn.

Border: Ch 1, sc around all 4 edges of this rectangle while working a ch-1 in each corner.

Fasten off, leaving a 16-inch (41-cm) tail for seaming.

Use this small rectangle to wrap around the center of the larger rectangle you just created and gather it in the center to create the bow shape. Stretch the smaller rectangle around the larger one until the two short ends meet. Use the tail to seam the short ends of the smaller rectangle together with a tapestry needle. Secure the smaller rectangle to the larger one by working your tapestry needle through both rectangle layers a few times to fasten them together. Fasten off, weave in ends.

Attaching Bow

Try on your sweater and place the bow at the bottom opening on the back of your sweater. Use stitch markers or scrap yarn to help mark your desired placement, centering it as best you can. With new yarn and a tapestry needle, seam the bow in place by stitching the perimeter of the bow to your sweater. There is approximately 6 to 8 inches (15 to 20 cm) of open space in the back of your sweater due to the back cutout. The bow will close this gap when secured across this opening. For some simple waist shaping, you can strategically pull in your sweater to hug your waist by pulling the two pieces from your back cutout (that were previously called Side 1 and Side 2) closer together, making the gap smaller, and seam your bow in place, securing your desired fit. (See the Bow section in Techniques on page 180 for photos and more instructions.)

Weave in any remaining ends, and block your sweater to the dimensions listed in the Sizing Chart (page 122).

A Lighter
Note

Lightweight Pieces for Any Season

In this chapter, we'll explore some lighter patterns designed for the warmer months. Each piece is made for light layering during the spring or fall, while Amber Magic Off-the-Shoulder Yoke (page 151) and Garnet Bay Cold-Shoulder (page 158) are perfect summer tops intended to be worn directly on the skin and not over another layer. Each design features a soft and sophisticated silhouette with uncomplicated stitch patterns for a clean, store-bought look. Most of these patterns combine a feminine element like wide sleeves or low necklines with playful details like bold striping or cheeky shaping.

Freshen up your wardrobe with a lightweight cardigan (page 137); an over-sized, breathable pullover (page 145); a cold-shoulder-style top (page 158); an off-the-shoulder circular yoke (page 151) and an elegant, bell-sleeve sweater (page 131). Make a design more summer friendly by choosing a breathable fiber, or by matching gauge with a yarn thinner than the pattern specifies.

Whether you're looking for something feminine and sweet or oversized and slouchy, this chapter has got you covered.

Emerald Valley
Bell-Sleeve Sweater

Emerald Valley features a modest neckline, bell sleeves and a classic fit that will stand the test of time. The feminine sleeves conform to the shape of your arm before gently widening at the wrist. This design was kept simple to showcase the beauty of these soft details and not overpower them.

Whether you're dressing for date night or business casual, this top can be worn on its own without being see-through and styled to suit almost any occasion. This straightforward, beginner-friendly design encourages customization—experiment with fiber choice, color or length to put your own spin on this sweater. The seasons may come and go, but the magic in these graceful sleeves is here to stay.

Construction

This sweater is worked in four pieces that are seamed together: two body panels and two identical sleeves. The front and back panels are worked bottom-up and partially seamed together, leaving openings for the sleeves. Next, the sleeves are worked separately from the top down in joined, turned rounds, while decreasing gradually down the arm and then increasing at the wrist to create the bell sleeves before being seamed onto the body.

Skill Level: Easy

Materials

Yarn:
DK—Lion Brand LB Collection Superwash Merino in Hunter (100% superwash Merino)
306 yds (280 m) per 3.5-oz (100-g) skein
Find this yarn on lionbrand.com or visit yarnsub.com to find comparable substitutes.

Yardage:
4 (5, 5, 6, 6) (7, 8, 8, 9) skeins or 1175 (1275, 1425, 1575, 1750) (1950, 2200, 2350, 2500) yds [1075 (1166, 1304, 1441, 1601) (1784, 2012, 2149, 2286) m]

Note: Budget friendly!
Lion Brand Superwash Merino is a lightweight, category #3 yarn, but if substituting, I would recommend using a sport weight (category #2) or even a heavy fingering weight (category #1) yarn that matches gauge for a close match to this lightweight DK.

Hook:
Size U.S. F/5 (3.75 mm) or size needed to obtain gauge

Notions:
Tapestry needle, several locking stitch markers

Gauge:
4 x 4" (10 x 10 cm) = 22 sts and 18 rows in half double crochet

ABBREVIATIONS

Written in U.S. crochet terms

ch: chain

FHDC: foundation half double crochet (see Foundation Stitches in the Techniques section on page 174)

hdc: half double crochet

hdc2tog: half double crochet 2 stitches together

rep: repeat

rnd(s): round(s)

sk: skip

sl st: slip stitch

st(s): stitch(es)

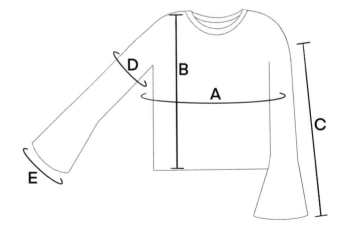

Emerald Valley Sizing Chart

	A FINISHED BUST CIRCUMFERENCE	B TOTAL LENGTH MEASURED FROM TOPS OF SHOULDERS	C SLEEVE LENGTH MEASURED FROM UNDERARM	D UPPER ARM CIRCUMFERENCE	E WRIST CIRCUMFERENCE
XS	36" 91 cm	19.5" 49 cm	18.5" 47 cm	11.5" 29 cm	14.5" 37 cm
S	40" 102 cm	19.5" 49 cm	17.5" 44 cm	12" 30 cm	15" 38 cm
M	44" 112 cm	21" 53 cm	16.5" 42 cm	12.75" 32 cm	15" 38 cm
L	48" 122 cm	22.5" 57 cm	15.5" 39 cm	14" 35 cm	15.25" 39 cm
XL	52" 132 cm	23.5" 60 cm	14.5" 37 cm	15.25" 39 cm	17" 43 cm
2X	56" 142 cm	24.5" 62 cm	14" 35 cm	17.25" 44 cm	18.25" 47 cm
3X	60" 152 cm	26" 66 cm	14" 35 cm	18.75" 48 cm	19.5" 49 cm
4X	64" 163 cm	27" 69 cm	12" 30 cm	20" 51 cm	21" 54 cm
5X	68" 173 cm	28" 71 cm	12" 30 cm	20" 51 cm	20.5" 52 cm

This chart shows the finished garment measurements. This sweater is designed to be worn with approximately 6 to 8 inches (15 to 20 cm) of positive ease. When choosing a size, find the bust measurement in this chart that equals approximately 6 to 8 inches (15 to 20 cm) larger than your actual bust measurement and make that size. For reference, the model is 5 feet, 4 inches (163 cm) tall with a 34-inch (86-cm) bust and is wearing a size small with a finished garment bust measurement of 40 inches (102 cm) with 6 inches (15 cm) of positive ease. If between sizes, size down.

For more information and tester photos, visit knitsnknots.ca/emerald-valley.

Emerald Valley Pattern

Back Panel

Row 1: Leaving a 24-inch (61-cm) tail for seaming, FHDC 99 (110, 121, 132, 143) (154, 165, 176, 187), turn.

Row 2: Ch 1, hdc in each st across, turn. [99 (110, 121, 132, 143) (154, 165, 176, 187) hdc]

Rep Row 2 until you have a total of 87 (87, 94, 101, 106) (111, 117, 122, 127) rows completed. If you matched gauge, this should measure approximately 19 (19, 21, 22.5, 23.5) (24.5, 26, 27, 28)" (48 [48, 53, 57, 60] [62, 66, 69, 71] cm).

> *Customization Tip:* For a longer (or shorter) sweater, work additional (or fewer) rows than instructed above. Make note of how many rows you added or eliminated so that you can make the same alteration to your front panel. Note that additional length will require additional yardage than listed for your size in the Materials section (page 131).

Fasten off.

Front Panel

Rep instructions from Row 1 and 2 of Back Panel.

Rep Row 2 until you have worked a total of 66 (66, 72, 77, 81) (85, 90, 94, 99) rows. If you matched gauge, this should be approximately 14.5 (14.5, 16, 17, 18) (19, 20, 21, 22)" (37 [37, 41, 43, 46] [48, 51, 53, 56] cm).

If you altered the length of the back panel, make the same alteration to the front panel instructions above.

Do not fasten off, continue with working yarn to Scoop Neck—First Side.

Scoop Neck—First Side

Row 1: Ch 1, hdc in next 32 (37, 42, 47, 52) (57, 62, 67, 72) sts, [hdc2tog] 2 times, turn. [34 (39, 44, 49, 54) (59, 64, 69, 74) hdc]

Row 2: Ch 1, [hdc2tog] 2 times, hdc to end of row, turn. [32 (37, 42, 47, 52) (57, 62, 67, 72) hdc]

Row 3: Ch 1, hdc in each st across until 2 sts remain unworked, hdc2tog, turn. [31 (36, 41, 46, 51) (56, 61, 66, 71) hdc]

Rows 4–21 (21, 22, 24, 25) (26, 27, 28, 28): Ch 1, hdc in each st across, turn.

Fasten off, leaving a 20-inch (51-cm) tail for seaming the tops of the shoulders.

Scoop Neck—Second Side

Lay work flat with Scoop Neck—First Side to your right. Count 36 (41, 46, 51, 56) (61, 66, 71, 76) sts from the unworked edge and attach new yarn into this st with a sl st.

Row 1: Ch 1, hdc in next st, hdc2tog, hdc to end of row, turn. [34 (39, 44, 49, 54) (59, 64, 69, 74) hdc]

Row 2: Ch 1, hdc in each st across until 4 sts remain unworked, [hdc2tog] 2 times, turn. [32 (37, 42, 47, 52) (57, 62, 67, 72) hdc]

Row 3: Ch 1, sk first st, hdc in next st and in each st across, turn. [31 (36, 41, 46, 51) (56, 61, 66, 71) hdc]

Rows 4–21 (21, 22, 24, 25) (26, 27, 28, 28): Ch 1, hdc in each st across, turn.

Fasten off, leaving a 20-inch (51-cm) tail for seaming the tops of the shoulders.

Partial Assembly

Lay the front panel over the back panel, aligning the sides stitch-for-stitch with interlocking stitch markers starting from the bottom and working your way up. Arrange your panels so that the long tails you left from your beginning foundation chains are on opposite sides.

With a tapestry needle and these long tails, seam the sides of your sweater using the whip stitch (see Techniques on page 167) or seaming method of your choice, starting from the bottom and stopping about 7 (7, 8, 8, 9) (10, 11, 12, 12)" (18 [18, 20, 20, 23] [25, 28, 30, 30] cm) from the tops of the shoulders, leaving this space open for attaching the sleeves.

With a tapestry needle and the long tails you left after finishing the Front Panel Scoop Neck, seam along the tops of the shoulders using the whip stitch or seaming method of your choice. Weave in ends.

Sleeves (Make 2)

You will begin the sleeves at the upper arm, decrease down toward the elbow, then increase at the wrist to create the elegant bell sleeves.

Rnd 1: Leaving a 24-inch (61-cm) tail for seaming the sleeve onto the body, FHDC 63 (66, 70, 76, 84) (95, 103, 110, 110), sl st into first FHDC to join round, turn. [63 (66, 70, 76, 84) (95, 103, 110, 110) FHDC]

Note: The sleeves are worked in joined rnds; remember to turn your work after each rnd to begin working in the opposite direction.

Rnd 2: Ch 1, hdc in each st around, sl st into first hdc to join rnd, turn.

For the remainder of the sleeve, work the rnds as specified for your size below:

When instructed to decrease, work the rnd as follows: Ch 1, hdc in first st, hdc2tog, hdc until 3 sts remain unworked, hdc2tog, hdc in last st, sl st into first hdc to join rnd, turn. [Decreases rnd by 2 sts]

When instructed to increase, work the rnd as follows: Ch 1, hdc in first st, 2 hdc in next st, hdc until 2 sts remain unworked, 2 hdc in next st, hdc in last st, sl st into first hdc to join rnd, turn. [Increases rnd by 2 sts]

All remaining rnds: Work every rnd that is not a decrease rnd nor increase rnd as a Rnd 2 rep.

Note: Total rnds provided include the first two rnds you have already completed.

Size XS: Hdc all sts until you have a total of 83 sleeve rnds completed, while decreasing in the following rnds: 15, 30, 45; then increasing in the following rnds: 51, 54, 57, 60, 63, 66, 69, 72, 75, 78, 81. [79 hdc]

Size S: Hdc all sts until you have a total of 78 sleeve rnds completed, decreasing in the following rnds: 10, 20, 30; then increasing in the following rnds: 46, 49, 52, 55, 58, 61, 64, 67, 70, 73, 76. [82 hdc]

Size M: Hdc all sts until you have a total of 74 sleeve rnds completed, decreasing in the following rnds: 10, 20, 30; then increasing in the following rnds: 41, 45, 49, 53, 57, 61, 65, 69, 73. [82 hdc]

Size L: Hdc all sts until you have a total of 69 sleeve rnds completed, decreasing in the following rnds: 8, 16, 24, 32; then increasing in the following rnds: 37, 41, 45, 49, 53, 57, 61, 65. [84 hdc]

Size 5X: Hdc all sts until you have a total of 54 sleeve rnds completed, while decreasing in the following rnds: 8, 16, 24; then increasing in the following rnds: 31, 37, 43, 49. [112 hdc]

Fasten off when the sleeve is complete.

Assembly

Lay the sleeves in place with the seams facing down toward the armpits. Use stitch markers to align the sleeves onto the body. Stretch the sleeves over the body sts slightly (approximately an inch [2.5 cm]) to avoid a tight sleeve seam. With a tapestry needle, use the tail from the foundation chain on each sleeve to loosely seam the sleeve to the body using the whip stitch or seaming method of your choice. Do not pull your yarn tight as you stitch or the seam will be tight and restricting. You want your seam to be loose so that your sleeve opening has some stretch, just like the rest of the sweater.

Return to the side seams you stitched earlier to close any remaining gaps at the underarm.

Weave in any remaining ends.

Neckline

Attach yarn to neckline with sl st at one of the shoulder seams.

Row 1: Ch 1, hdc evenly around neckline, sl st into first hdc to join rnd, turn.

Row 2: Ch 1, hdc in each st around, sl st into first hdc to join rnd.

Fasten off, weave in any remaining ends and block your sweater to the dimensions listed in the Sizing Chart (page 133).

Size XL: Hdc all sts until you have a total of 65 sleeve rnds completed, decreasing in the following rnds: 8, 16, 24; then increasing in the following rnds: 34, 38, 42, 46, 50, 54, 58, 62. [94 hdc]

Size 2X: Hdc all sts until you have a total of 63 sleeve rnds completed, decreasing in the following rnds: 8, 16, 24; then increasing in the following rnds: 35, 40, 45, 50, 55, 60. [101 hdc]

Size 3X: Hdc all sts until you have a total of 63 sleeve rnds completed, decreasing in the following rnds: 8, 16, 24; then increasing in the following rnds: 33, 39, 45, 51, 57. [107 hdc]

Size 4X: Hdc all sts until you have a total of 58 sleeve rnds completed, decreasing in the following rnds: 8, 16, 24; then increasing in the following rnds: 31, 36, 41, 46. [112 hdc]

Mountain Peaks
Cardigan

Ease your way into making your own clothes with this truly beginner-friendly pattern. Beginners and seasoned crocheters alike are sure to be pleasantly surprised by this polished finished piece, created using just the half double crochet stitch and minimal shaping.

The color combinations for this color-block cardigan are endless—feel free to make up your own striping pattern or opt for one solid color for a wearable cardigan that speaks to your personal style. Whether you're lounging at home or out and about, this chic layering piece is destined to become a part of your regular outfit rotation. With its easygoing fit, this refined, can-be-worn-with-anything cardigan is the ultimate grab-and-go piece.

Construction

The Mountain Peaks Cardigan is worked from the bottom up in five separate pieces: one back panel, two identical front panels and two sleeves. The body panels begin with the bottom hem, and the sleeves begin with the cuff. The sleeves are worked seamlessly in joined rounds and then seamed onto the body.

Materials

Yarn:
DK—The Hook Nook Small Stuff in Blue Steel, Minimalist, Foggy Morning (100% acrylic)
273 yds (250 m) per 3.5-oz (100-g) skein

Yardage for 3-color cardigan like sample shown:
Color A (bottom)—Blue Steel: 2 (2, 2, 2, 3) (3, 3, 3, 3) skeins or 445 (480, 515, 545, 585) (615, 650, 700, 745) yds [407 (439, 471, 499, 535) (563, 595, 641, 682) m]

ABBREVIATIONS
Written in U.S. crochet terms
ch: chain
hdc: half double crochet
hdc2tog: half double crochet 2 stitches together
rep: repeat
rnd(s): round(s)
sl st: slip stitch
st(s): stitch(es)

Color B (middle)—Minimalist: 3 (3, 3, 3, 3) (4, 4, 4, 4) skeins or 550 (580, 635, 675, 750) (800, 850, 920, 925) yds [503 (531, 581, 618, 686) (732, 778, 842, 846) m]

Color C (top)—Foggy Morning: 2 (2, 2, 2, 2) (2, 3, 3, 3) skeins or 420 (445, 480, 510, 525) (535, 580, 615, 660) yds [385 (407, 439, 467, 481) (490, 531, 563, 604) m]

Yardage for 1-color cardigan: 6 (6, 6, 7, 7) (8, 8, 9, 9) skeins or 1400 (1500, 1625, 1725, 1850) (1950, 2075, 2225, 2325) yds [1281 (1372, 1486, 1578, 1692) (1784, 1898, 2035, 2126) m]

Substitute Small Stuff with any similar DK weight, category #3 yarn that matches gauge. Any fiber content should produce a beautiful cardigan!

Hook:
Size U.S. G/7 (4.5 mm) or size needed to obtain gauge

Notions:
Tapestry needle, several locking stitch markers for seaming

Gauge:
4 x 4" (10 x 10 cm) = 17 sts and 12 rows in half double crochet

Mountain Peaks Sizing Chart

	A FINISHED BUST CIRCUMFERENCE	BUILT-IN POSITIVE EASE	B TOTAL LENGTH MEASURED FROM TOPS OF SHOULDERS	C SLEEVE LENGTH MEASURED FROM UNDERARM	D UPPER ARM CIRCUMFERENCE	E WRIST CIRCUMFERENCE
XS	35.5" 90 cm	5.5–7.5" 14–19 cm	28" 71 cm	20" 51 cm	10.25" 26 cm	8.5" 22 cm
S	39.5" 100 cm	5.5–7.5" 14–19 cm	28" 71 cm	19" 48 cm	11.25" 29 cm	8.5" 22 cm
M	44" 112 cm	6–8" 15–20 cm	28" 71 cm	18" 46 cm	11.75" 30 cm	8.5" 22 cm
L	46.5" 118 cm	4.5–6.5" 11–17 cm	28" 71 cm	18" 46 cm	12.75" 32 cm	8.5" 22 cm
XL	51" 130 cm	5–7" 13–18 cm	28" 71 cm	16.75" 43 cm	14.25" 36 cm	9" 23 cm
2X	55" 140 cm	5–7" 13–18 cm	28" 71 cm	16" 41 cm	16.25" 41 cm	9" 23 cm
3X	59" 150 cm	5–7" 13–18 cm	28" 71 cm	15.5" 39 cm	17.75" 45 cm	9" 23 cm
4X	63.5" 161 cm	5.5–7.5" 14–19 cm	28" 71 cm	14" 36 cm	19.25" 49 cm	10" 25 cm
5X	68" 173 cm	6–8" 15–20 cm	28" 71 cm	13" 33 cm	19.25" 49 cm	10" 25 cm

This chart shows the finished garment measurements. This cardigan is designed to be worn with up to 8 inches (20 cm) of positive ease, depending on the size you are making. Find the finished bust measurement in this chart and refer to the built-in ease when choosing a size to make. For reference, the model is 5 feet, 4 inches (163 cm) tall with a 34-inch (86-cm) bust and is wearing a size small with a finished garment bust measurement of 39.5 inches (100 cm) worn with 5.5 inches (14 cm) of positive ease. If between sizes, size down.

For more information and tester photos, visit knitsnknots.ca/mountain-peaks.

Mountain Peaks Pattern

Schematic

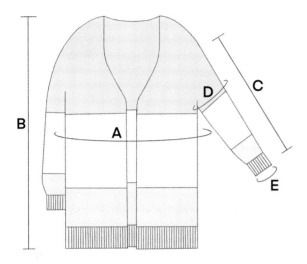

Back Panel

Bottom Hem

Using Color A, ch 21.

Row 1: Hdc in 2nd ch from hook and in each ch across, turn. [20 hdc]

Row 2: Ch 1, hdc in each hdc across, turn.

Rep Row 2 until you have a total of 50 (56, 62, 66, 72) (78, 84, 90, 96) rows completed.

Turn your work to begin working across the ends of the rows you just completed.

Body

Row 1: Ch 1, *work 3 hdc for every 2 row-ends; rep from * across the entire length of the bottom hem, turn. [75 (84, 93, 99, 108) (117, 126, 135, 144) hdc]

Rows 2–70: Ch 1, hdc in each st to end of row, turn, while working the following color changes:

Rows 1–14: Color A

Rows 15–42: Color B

Rows 43–70: Color C

> *Customization Tip:* For a shorter (or longer) cardigan than the length provided in the Sizing Chart (page 138), work fewer (or additional) rows than instructed. To keep the color-block proportions consistent, eliminate (or add) rows in multiples of three, one from each color-block section. Note that adding length requires more yardage than listed in the Materials section (page 137).

Fasten off, block if desired.

Front Panel (Make 2)

Bottom Hem

Using Color A, ch 21.

Row 1: Hdc in 2nd ch from hook and in each ch across, turn. [20 hdc]

Row 2: Ch 1, hdc in each hdc across, turn.

Rep Row 2 until you have a total of 26 (28, 32, 34, 36) (38, 42, 44, 48) rows completed.

Turn your work to begin working across the ends of the rows you just completed.

Body

Row 1: Ch 1, *work 3 hdc for every 2 row-ends; rep from * across the entire length of the bottom hem, turn. [39 (42, 48, 51, 54) (57, 63, 66, 72) hdc]

Row 2: Ch 1, hdc in each hdc across, turn.

Note that if you adjusted the length of your back panel, work the same adjustments to your front panels to keep your color-blocking consistent.

Rep Row 2 until you have a total of 46 (48, 46, 46, 48) (48, 46, 48, 46) rows completed, while working the following color changes:
Rows 1–14: Color A

Rows 15–42: Color B

Rows 43–46 or 48 as indicated by instructions above for your size: Color C

Continuing with Color C

Next Row: Ch 1, hdc in each st until 3 sts remain unworked, hdc2tog, hdc in last st, turn. [decreases row by 1 st] [38 (41, 47, 50, 53) (56, 62, 65, 71) hdc]

Next Row: Ch 1, hdc in each st to end of row, turn.

Rep last 2 rows 11 (10, 11, 11, 10) (10, 11, 10, 11) more times. [27 (31, 36, 39, 43) (46, 51, 55, 60) hdc]

You will finish with a total of 70 rows completed. Fasten off, leaving a long tail for seaming the tops of the shoulders. Block if desired.

Sleeves (Make 2)

Sleeve Cuff

Using Color A, ch 16, leaving an 8-inch (20-cm) tail for seaming cuff closed.

Row 1: Hdc in 2nd ch from hook and in each ch across, turn. [15 hdc]

Row 2: Ch 1, hdc in each hdc across, turn.

Rep Row 2 until you have a total of 24 (24, 24, 24, 26) (26, 26, 28, 28) rows completed.

Turn your work to begin working across the ends of the rows you just completed.

Sleeve Body

Rnd 1: Ch 1, *work 3 hdc for every 2 row-ends; rep from * across the entire length of your sleeve cuff, sl st into first hdc to join rnd, turn. [36 (36, 36, 36, 39) (39, 39, 42, 42) hdc]

With a tapestry needle and the tail from your beginning ch, seam the cuff closed using the whip stitch (see Techniques on page 167) or seaming method of your choice.

Note: The remainder of the sleeve is worked in back-and-forth joined rnds. Make sure to turn your work after each rnd.

For the remainder of the sleeve, work the rnds as specified for your size below:

When instructed to increase, work the rnd as follows: Ch 1, hdc in first hdc, 2 hdc in next hdc, hdc in each st until 2 sts remain unworked, 2 hdc in next st, hdc in last st, sl st into first hdc to join rnd, turn. [Increases rnd by 2 sts]

Work all non-increase rnds as follows: Ch 1, hdc in each st to end of row, sl st into first hdc to join rnd, turn.

Notes: Total rnds provided includes the first rnd you have already completed.

As you work the following increase rnds, be mindful of where the color changes take place.

XS: Work a total of 50 rnds, while working the following rnds as increase rnds: 10, 20, 30, 40. Begin Color B in rnd 12, begin Color C in rnd 39. [44 hdc]

S: Work a total of 47 rnds, while working the following rnds as increase rnds: 7, 14, 21, 28, 35, 42. Begin Color B in rnd 12, begin Color C in rnd 39. [48 hdc]

M: Work a total of 44 rnds, while working the following rnds as increase rnds: 6, 12, 18, 24, 30, 36, 42. Begin Color B in rnd 10, begin Color C in rnd 37. [50 hdc]

L: Work a total of 43 rnds, while working the following rnds as increase rnds: 5, 9, 13, 17, 21, 25, 29, 33, 37. Begin Color B in rnd 10, begin Color C in rnd 37. [54 hdc]

XL: Work a total of 40 rnds, while working the following rnds as increase rnds: 2, 5, 8, 11, 14, 17, 20, 23, 26, 29, 32. Begin Color B in rnd 10, begin Color C in rnd 36. [61 hdc]

2X: Work a total of 38 rnds, while working the following rnds as increase rnds: 2, 4, 6, 8, 10, 12, 14, 16, 18, 20, 22, 24, 26, 28, 30. Begin Color B in rnd 10, begin Color C in rnd 34. [69 hdc]

3X: Work a total of 36 rnds, while working the following rnds as increase rnds: 2, 4, 6, 8, 10, 12, 14, 16, 18, 20, 22, 24, 26, 28, 30, 32, 34, 36. Begin Color B in rnd 8, begin Color C in rnd 32. [75 hdc]

4X (5X): Work a total of 32 (29) rnds, while working the following rnds as increase rnds: 2–21. Begin Color B in rnd 8 (8), begin Color C in rnd 30 (27). [82 (82) hdc]

Fasten off, leaving a 30-inch (76-cm) tail for seaming the sleeves to the body panels.

Assembly

Lay the front panels over the back panel with the decrease edges toward the middle. Use locking stitch markers to help line up the panels stitch-for-stitch along the shoulders and sides of the cardigan as best you can.

With a tapestry needle, seam the sides of your cardigan using the whip stitch or seaming method of your choice, starting from the bottom hem. Seam about three-quarters of the way up, leaving plenty of room for attaching the sleeves. Rep for both sides of the cardigan.

Seam the tops of the shoulders using the tails from your front panels.

Place the finished sleeves at the armholes with the sleeve seams pointing down toward the armpits and use locking stitch markers to align the stitches evenly around the sleeve openings on the body panels. Use the tail end to seam the sleeve in place using the whip stitch or seaming method of your choice. When seaming the sleeves onto your cardigan, make sure to keep this seam loose (do not pull tight) to maintain some stretch, otherwise this seam will restrict your arms during wear. Use the tail from the side seam to close any remaining gaps. Weave in ends.

Finishing Row

There is one finishing row around the collar of the cardigan to make the raw edges look neater. Starting at one bottom inside corner of your cardigan, you will work up and around the neckline, and back down to the opposite bottom inside corner.

Using Color A, attach new yarn with a sl st to the inside corner of the cardigan along the bottom hem. Ch 1, hdc into each hdc from bottom hem, then work 3 hdc for every 2 row-ends, changing colors when necessary to match the colors used in your body panels, while working 1 hdc into each st along the back-neck. Once you reach the bottom hem on the opposite side of your cardigan, hdc into each hdc until reaching the opposite bottom corner.

Fasten off, weave in any remaining ends and block your sweater to the dimensions listed in the Sizing Chart (page 138).

Customization Tips: This cardigan is a basic design, leaving a lot of opportunities to personalize it and make it more "you." To further customize this cardigan, try working additional design elements such as decorative buttons down the front, belt loops and a long waist tie, more "finishing rows" for a thicker border around the collar, front pockets* or anything else you'd like to add!

*Instructions for optional belt loops, waist tie and front pockets included below.

To add pockets, follow these instructions or use them as a guideline:

Pocket

Top Border

Ch 7.

Row 1: Hdc in 2nd ch from hook and in each ch across, turn. [6 hdc]

Row 2: Ch 1, hdc in each st across, turn.

Rep Row 2 until desired pocket width, finishing on an even-numbered row.

Turn your work to begin working across the ends of the rows you just completed.

Main Pocket

Row 1: Ch 1, *work 3 hdc for every 2 row-ends; rep from * across the entire length of your border, turn.

Row 2: Ch 1, hdc in each st across, turn.

Rep Row 2 until you have reached your desired pocket depth. Fasten off, block if desired, and seam to your cardigan with a tapestry needle in your desired placement. See page 178 for help with seaming a pocket to a finished garment.

To add belt loops and a waist tie, follow these instructions or use them as a guideline:

Waist Tie

Work a short chain that equals 1 chain longer than your desired waist-tie width, turn.

Row 1: Hdc in 2nd ch from hook and in each ch across, turn.

Row 2: Ch 1, hdc in each st across, turn.

Rep Row 2 until you reach your desired waist-tie length.

Belt Loops

With new yarn, work a ch slightly longer than your tie is thick. (For example, if your tie is 3 inches [8 cm] wide, then your chain needs to be slightly longer than 3 inches [8 cm].)

Row 1: Hdc in 2nd ch from hook and in each ch across, turn.

Row 2: Ch 1, hdc in each st across, turn.

Fasten off, leaving a tail for seaming the belt loop onto your cardigan. Use a tapestry needle and the two tail ends of the belt loop to seam in place on the sides of the cardigan or in your desired placement.

Rep for 1 belt loop on each side, or as many times as desired.

Timber Lodge
Striped Pullover

The inspiration for Timber Lodge—a whimsical, vintage-inspired sweater—came from a 1970s heirloom blanket. Featuring an oversized fit and drop-shoulder sleeves, you'll love the laid-back feel of this sweater and the way it gently contours to your body.

Crochet in the 1970s often consisted of bright colors, bold patterns and simple shapes. With this in mind, I paired some bold striping with a shade of mustard often seen in clothing at this time, all on a natural, cream background. In keeping with the '70s theme, I accentuated the look of distinct crochet rows, the structure of the individual stitches further emphasized at each color transition. Intended to look like a vintage piece that has been passed down in the family, I hope Timber Lodge sparks a feeling of comfort, familiarity and nostalgia. Maybe you'll pass it down to the next generation, like a true heirloom piece.

Construction

This sweater is worked in three pieces: one body and two identical sleeves. There is very little seaming in this sweater because each piece is worked in joined rounds. The body is worked in one piece from the bottom up, then splits to work the front and back and create space for the sleeves. The sleeves are worked from the bottom up and seamed to the body. Last, ribbing is worked along the neckline.

Materials

Yarn:
Sport—WeCrochet Paragon Sport in White (Main Color), Black (Accent Color A), Turmeric (Accent Color B) (50% fine Merino wool, 25% baby alpaca, 25% mulberry silk)

123 yds (117 m) per 1.8-oz (50-g) ball

Find this yarn on crochet.com or visit yarnsub.com to find comparable substitutes.

Yardage (3-tone):
Main Color: 8 (9, 9, 10, 11) (12, 13, 14, 14) balls or 900 (1000, 1075, 1200, 1300) (1450, 1550, 1625, 1700) yds [823 (915, 983, 1098, 1189) (1326, 1418, 1486, 1555) m]
Accent Color A: 7 (7, 7, 8, 9) (9, 9, 9, 10) balls or 775 (800, 850, 925, 975) (1000, 1050, 1100, 1150) yds [709 (732, 778, 846, 892) (915, 961, 1006, 1052) m]
Accent Color B: 2 (3, 3, 3, 3) (3, 3, 4, 4) balls or 225 (250, 275, 300, 325) (350, 375, 400, 425) yds [206 (229, 252, 275, 298) (321, 343, 366, 389) m]
Yardage (solid color): 16 (17, 18, 20, 22) (23, 25, 26, 27) balls or 1900 (2050, 2200, 2425, 2600) (2800, 2975, 3125, 3275) yds [1738 (1875, 2012, 2218, 2378) (2561, 2721, 2858, 2995) m]

Note: Budget-friendly alternatives include WeCrochet Swish DK, WeCrochet Shine Sport, WeCrochet Galileo, Lion Brand Coboo, Lion Brand Truboo.

Substitute WeCrochet Paragon Sport with any similar sport weight, category #2 yarn that matches gauge. This particular yarn is bouncy from the wool, with a slight sheen and a very prominent twist. Paragon is a more luxurious fiber, and it can get a bit pricy to make a full garment with it. Any sport weight yarn can be used in place of Paragon and still produce a beautiful sweater that you'll love to wear.

Hook:
Size U.S. E/4 (3.5 mm) or size needed to obtain gauge

Notions:
Tapestry needle, several locking stitch markers

Gauge:
4 x 4" (10 x 10 cm) = 18 sts and 15 rows in half double crochet

ABBREVIATIONS
Written in U.S. crochet terms
ch: chain
hdc: half double crochet
PM: place marker
rep: repeat
rnd: round
sc: single crochet
scBLO: single crochet in the back loop only
sk: skip
sl st: slip stitch
st(s): stitch(es)
tch: turning chain

Schematic

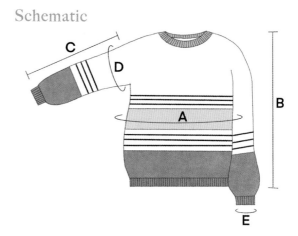

Timber Lodge Sizing Chart

	A FINISHED BUST CIRCUMFERENCE	B TOTAL LENGTH MEASURED FROM TOPS OF SHOULDERS	C SLEEVE LENGTH MEASURED FROM UNDERARM	D UPPER ARM CIRCUMFERENCE	E WRIST CIRCUMFERENCE
XS	40" 102 cm	22" 56 cm	18" 46 cm	12.75" 32 cm	8.5" 22 cm
S	44" 112 cm	22" 56 cm	17" 43 cm	13.25" 34 cm	9" 23 cm
M	48" 122 cm	22.5" 57 cm	16.25" 41 cm	14" 36 cm	9.25" 23 cm
L	52" 132 cm	22.5" 57 cm	15.5" 39 cm	15.25" 39 cm	10.25" 26 cm
XL	56" 142 cm	23" 58 cm	15" 38 cm	16.25" 41 cm	10.25" 26 cm
2X	60" 152 cm	24" 61 cm	14" 36 cm	18.5" 47 cm	10.25" 26 cm
3X	64" 163 cm	24" 61 cm	13.25" 34 cm	19" 48 cm	10.25" 26 cm
4X	68" 173 cm	24" 61 cm	13" 33 cm	20" 51 cm	10.75" 27 cm
5X	72" 183 cm	24" 61 cm	13" 33 cm	20" 51 cm	10.75" 27 cm

This chart shows the finished garment measurements. This sweater is designed to be worn with approximately 10 to 12 inches (25 to 30 cm) of positive ease. When choosing a size, find the bust measurement in this chart that equals approximately 10 to 12 inches (25 to 30 cm) larger than your actual bust measurement and make this size. For reference, the model is 5 feet, 4 inches (163 cm) tall with a 34-inch (86-cm) bust and is wearing a size small with a finished garment bust measurement of 44 inches (112 cm) with 10 inches (25 cm) of positive ease. For more information and tester photos, visit knitsnknots.ca/timber-lodge.

Timber Lodge Pattern

Body
Bottom Ribbing
Use Accent Color A

Ch 25, leaving a 12-inch (30-cm) tail for seaming.

Row 1: Sc in second ch from hook and in each ch across, turn. [24 sc]

Row 2: Ch 1, sc in first st, scBLO in each st until 1 st remains, sc in last st, turn.

Rep Row 2 until you have worked a total of 180 (198, 216, 234, 252) (270, 288, 306, 324) rows.

After last row, turn work to begin working into the edges of the rows you just completed.

The body will be worked in joined, turned rnds. Remember to sl st into the first st of the row to join in the rnd, then turn your work to begin a new rnd.

Body
Rnd 1: Ch 1, work 1 sc into the ends of each row you just completed, sl st into first sc to join rnd, turn. [180 (198, 216, 234, 252) (270, 288, 306, 324) sc]

Use the tail from the beginning ch to seam the first and last rows of ribbing together using the whip stitch (page 167) or seaming method of your choice.

Rnd 2: Ch 1, hdc in each st to end of rnd, sl st into first hdc to join, turn. [180 (198, 216, 234, 252) (270, 288, 306, 324) hdc]

Rnds 3–6: Rep Row 2.

Note on Changing Colors: When working the last stitch of an old color, work the stitch as usual, but use the new color to do your final yarn-over and pull through to close the stitch. Then, you may cut the old color and continue stitching with the new color.

Change to Main Color
Rnds 7–9: Rep Rnd 2.

Change to Accent Color A
Rnd 10: Ch 1, sc in each st to end of rnd, sl st into first sc to join, turn.

Rnd 11: Ch 1, sc into the st below (the same st you worked into in Rnd 10) to end of rnd, sl st into first sc to join, turn.

Change to Main Color
Rnds 12–13: Rep Rnd 2.

Rnds 14–21: Rep Rnds 10–13 two more times, changing colors where indicated.

Continuing with Main Color
Rnd 22: Rep Rnd 2.

Change to Accent Color B
Rnds 23–40: Rep Rnd 2.

Rnds 41–55: Rep Rnds 7–21, changing colors where indicated.

Continuing with Main Color
Rnds 56–61: Rep Rnd 2.

This is where you will begin splitting the work into front and back panels and making room for the sleeves. The length of your work so far is the measurement from your underarm to the bottom of your sweater. For a shorter (or longer) sweater, work fewer (or additional) Row 2 reps using your main color until satisfied with the length from the underarm, then proceed to Front.

Front
Row 1: Sl st into next 4 (4, 5, 6, 7) (8, 9, 10, 11) sts, ch 1, hdc in next st, PM in this hdc to help identify first st of row, hdc in next 81 (90, 97, 104, 111) (118, 125, 132, 139) sts, turn.

Rows 2–7: Ch 1, hdc in each st across, turn. [82 (91, 98, 105, 112) (117, 126, 133, 140) hdc]
You are now going to split this front piece into Side 1 and Side 2 to create a neck opening.

Lay your work with the front side facing up and the completed side on the right. Starting from the left side of Front Side 1, count 26 (25, 26, 25, 26) (27, 28, 29, 28) sts toward the left, leaving these sts unworked and join yarn with a sl st in the next st.

Row 8: Ch 1, hdc in same st as sl st and in each st across, turn. [28 (33, 36, 40, 43) (46, 49, 52, 56) hdc]

Row 9: Ch 1, hdc in each st across until 2 sts remain, sk next st, hdc in last st, turn. [27 (32, 35, 39, 42) (45, 48, 51, 55) hdc]

Row 10: Ch 1, sk first st, hdc in next st and each st across, turn. [26 (31, 34, 38, 41) (44, 47, 50, 54) hdc]

Row 11: Rep Row 9. [25 (30, 33, 37, 40) (43, 46, 49, 53) hdc]

Next 10 (11, 12, 13, 14) (17, 18, 18, 18) rows: Ch 1, hdc in each st across, turn.

Fasten off, leaving a 20-inch (51-cm) tail for seaming the shoulders.

Front side is complete.

Back

You are now going to work the back panel in a similar way, working into the unworked sts from Row 61. Lay the work with the front of the sweater facing down, and the unworked back side facing up. The side seam should be to the left. You may have to turn your work inside out to achieve this orientation. Count 4 (4, 5, 6, 7) (8, 9, 10, 11) sts from seam and PM in this st. You will come back to this. Move to the opposite side of your sweater (the side without the seam) on your right at the front panel edge. Count 8 (8, 10, 12, 14) (16, 18, 20, 22) sts from front edge, and leave these sts unworked. Insert your hook into the next st and join yarn with a sl st.

Row 1: Ch 1, hdc in same st as sl st and in each st across, stopping at the st right before the marker, turn. You can remove the marker. [82 (91, 98, 105, 112) (117, 126, 133, 140) hdc]

Front—Side 1

Row 8: Ch 1, hdc in next 28 (33, 36, 40, 43) (46, 49, 52, 56) sts, turn. [28 (33, 36, 40, 43) (46, 49, 52, 56) hdc]

Row 9: Ch 1, sk first st, hdc in next st and each st across, turn. [27 (32, 35, 39, 42) (45, 48, 51, 55) hdc]

Row 10: Ch 1, hdc in each st across until 2 sts remain, sk next st, hdc in last st, turn. [26 (31, 34, 38, 41) (44, 47, 50, 54) hdc]

Row 11: Rep Row 9. [25 (30, 33, 37, 40) (43, 46, 49, 53) hdc]

Next 10 (11, 12, 13, 14) (17, 18, 18, 18) rows: Ch 1, hdc in each st across, turn.

Fasten off, leaving a 20-inch (51-cm) tail for seaming the shoulders.

Rows 2–16 (17, 18, 19, 20) (23, 24, 24, 24): Ch 1, hdc in each st across, turn.

Do not fasten off, continue to Back Side 1 using same yarn.

Back—Side 1
Next 5 rows: Ch 1, hdc in next 25 (30, 33, 37, 40) (43, 46, 49, 53) sts, turn. [25 (30, 33, 37, 40) (43, 46, 49, 53) hdc]

Fasten off.

Back—Side 2
Count 25 (30, 33, 37, 40) (43, 46, 49, 53) sts from unworked edge and join yarn with a sl st into this st.

Next 5 rows: Ch 1, hdc in next 25 (30, 33, 37, 40) (43, 46, 49, 53) sts, turn. [25 (30, 33, 37, 40) (43, 46, 49, 53) hdc]

Fasten off.

Use tails from Front Side 1 and 2 to seam the tops of the shoulders with a tapestry needle using the whip stitch or seaming method of your choice. Weave in ends.

Sleeves (Make 2)
Bottom Ribbing
Using Accent Color A, ch 15, leaving a 12-inch (30-cm) tail for seaming the sleeve cuff ribbing.

Row 1: Sc in 2nd ch from hook and in each ch across, turn. [14 sc]

Row 2: Ch 1, sc in first sc, scBLO in next 12 sts, sc in last st, turn.

Rep Row 2 until you have worked a total of 38 (40, 42, 46, 46) (46, 46, 48, 48) rows.

After last row, turn work to begin working into the edges of the rows you just completed.

Both sleeves will be worked in joined rnds, turning work after each rnd.

Rnd 1: Ch 1, work 1 sc into the ends of each row you just completed, sl st into first sc to join rnd, turn. [38 (40, 42, 46, 46) (46, 46, 48, 48) sc]

Use the tail from the beginning ch to seam the first and last rows of ribbing together using the whip stitch or seaming method of your choice.

Rnd 2: Ch 1, hdc in each st to end of rnd, sl st into first hdc to join, turn. [38 (40, 42, 46, 46) (46, 46, 48, 48) hdc]

Rnd 3: Ch 1, *hdc in first st, 2 hdc in next st; rep from * to end of rnd, sl st into first hdc to join, turn. [57 (60, 63, 69, 69) (69, 69, 72, 72) hdc]

Rnds 4–17: Rep Rnd 2.

Change to Main Color
XS, S, M and L only: Rnds 18–20: Rep Rnd 2.

XL, 2X, 3X, 4X and 5X only: Rnd 18: Ch 1, hdc in first st, 2 hdc in next st, hdc in each st around until 2 sts remain, 2 hdc in next st, hdc in last st, sl st to join, turn. [x (x, x, x, 71) (71, 71, 74, 74) hdc]

XL, 2X, 3X, 4X and 5X only: Rnds 19–20: Rep Rnd 2.

Change to Accent Color A

Rnd 21: Ch 1, sc in each st to end of rnd, sl st to join, turn.

Rnd 22: Ch 1, sc into the st below (the same st you worked into in Rnd 21) to end of rnd, sl st into first sc to join, turn.

Change to Main Color

Rnds 23–24: Rep Rnd 2.

Rnds 25–32: Rep Rnds 21–24 two more times, changing colors where indicated.

Continuing with Main Color for the remainder of the sleeve

Rnd 33: Rep Rnd 2.

XS, S, M and L only:
Rnds 34–68 (64, 61, 58): Rep Rnd 2.

For shorter (or longer) sleeves than written for your size, work fewer (or additional) Rnd 2 reps here.

XL only:
Rnd 34: Rep Rnd 18. [73 hdc]

Rnds 35–56: Rep Rnd 2.

For shorter (or longer) sleeves than written for your size, work fewer (or additional) Rnd 2 reps here.

2X (3X, 4X, 5X) only:
Rnd 34: Rep Rnd 18. [73 (73, 76, 76) hdc]

Next 2 (1, 1, 1) rnds: Rep Rnd 2.

Rep [**Rnd 34 and the 2 (1, 1, 1) rnds that follow**] five (six, seven, seven) times. [83 (85, 90, 90) hdc]

Hdc all sts for the next 2 (3, 0, 0) rnds.
For shorter (or longer) sleeves than written for your size, work fewer (or additional) Rnd 2 reps where you see fit.

At this point, your sleeve should have a total of 68 (64, 61, 58, 56) (53, 50, 49, 49) rnds worked after the cuff ribbing.

Fasten off, leaving a 24-inch (61-cm) tail for seaming the sleeve to the body of your sweater.

Assembly

Determine which side of your Body and Sleeves you would like to wear as the "right side." Place the sleeves at the armhole openings with the right side of all pieces facing you and the sleeve seams facing down toward the armpits. Stretch the sleeves over the openings slightly (about 1 inch [2.5 cm] or so) and pin in place using locking stitch markers. Loosely seam the sleeves in place using the whip stitch or seaming method of your choice and close any gaps. Make sure not to pull tight when seaming the sleeves onto the body, otherwise, the sleeve opening will feel restricting during wear.

Neckline

Using Main Color

With the right side facing, attach yarn to the neckline with a sl st at one of the shoulder seams.

Set-Up Row: Ch 1, sc evenly around neckline, sl st into first sc to join rnd.

Change to Accent Color A or desired color

Ch 10.

Row 1: Sc in 2nd ch from hook and in each ch across, sl st in next 2 sts from Set-Up Row, turn. [9 sc]

Row 2: [No tch] Sk the 2 sl st just made in Set-Up Row, scBLO in next 8 sts, sc in last st, turn.

Row 3: Ch 1, sc in first st, scBLO in next 8 sts, sl st in next 2 sts from Set-Up Row, turn.

Rep Rows 2–3 until you have worked your way across the entire Set-Up Row. Cut yarn and use the tail to seam the first and last rows of the neckline ribbing together with a tapestry needle using the whip stitch or seaming method of your choice. Weave in any remaining ends and block your sweater to the dimensions listed in the Sizing Chart (page 146).

Amber Magic

Off-the-Shoulder Yoke

A lightweight, more poised version of the Sugarplum Off-the-Shoulder Yoke (page 105), Amber Magic is crocheted with an identical construction using a luxurious fingering weight yarn. Demonstrating how yarn choice can totally transform a design, I wanted to include both a bulky weight and fingering weight version of this sweater, each one producing a completely unique fabric to mix with different outfits, suitable for different occasions. This delicate, airy version offers an entirely different drape and sophistication despite sharing an identical construction.

Equally playful and poised, this off-the-shoulder sweater was designed with a stretch-less neckline so you can wear this piece with confidence knowing it won't slip off your shoulders. Keep it centered to expose both shoulders, or shift it off one shoulder to flaunt a tasteful, slouchy look. The three-quarter-length sleeves are fitted in the upper arm and transition to a more relaxed fit. I recommend wearing this sweater on its own with a strapless bra or wearing this piece over a tank top or dress for a peek-a-boo, layered effect.

Construction

This sweater has a circular yoke construction, worked seamlessly from the top down. After completing the yoke increases, the yoke is then separated to create space for the body and the sleeves. The body is worked next, and the sleeves are worked last.

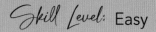

Skill Level: Easy

Materials

Yarn:
Fingering—WeCrochet Gloss Fingering in Harvest (70% Merino wool, 30% silk)
220 yds (200 m) per 1.8-oz (50-g) hank
Find this yarn on crochet.com or visit yarnsub.com to find comparable substitutes.

Yardage:
7 (8, 8, 9, 9) (10, 11, 12, 13) hanks or 1275 (1425, 1600, 1775, 2025) (2250, 2350, 2725, 2825) yds [1166 (1304, 1463, 1623, 1852) (2058, 2149, 2492, 2584] m]

Note on Yardage: Yardage is for a slightly cropped sweater and three-quarter-length sleeves as shown in the sample and the Sizing Chart (page 152). Additional yardage will be needed if you would like a full-length sweater or longer sleeves.

Note: Budget friendly!
Substitute Gloss Fingering with any similar fingering weight, category #1 yarn that matches gauge. Any fiber should work out fine, just be mindful of how much your chosen fiber grows upon blocking or washing.

Yarn Note: This design is comprised of center single crochet stitches throughout, encouraging you to get creative with your yarn choices. Simple stitches like this are great opportunities to use any special, unique yarns you may have on hand that you want to show off without getting lost in a distracting stitch pattern. Speckled, variegated, self-striping and hand-dyed yarns pair best with a blank canvas of simple stitches to really let the yarn shine.

Hook:
Size U.S. G/6 (4 mm) or size needed to obtain gauge
Note: 4 mm hooks are sometimes labeled as F/5, and sometimes G/6.

Notions:
Tapestry needle, five locking stitch markers

Gauge:
4 x 4" (10 x 10 cm) = 16 sts and 23 rows in center single crochet worked in the round

Amber Magic Sizing Chart

	A FINISHED BUST CIRCUMFER-ENCE	B NECK OPEN-ING CIRCUMFER-ENCE	C YOKE DEPTH MEASURED FROM FIRST YOKE ROUND TO LAST YOKE ROUND	D LENGTH OF BODY MEASURED FROM UNDERARM	E UPPER ARM CIRCUMFER-ENCE	F LOWER SLEEVE CIRCUMFER-ENCE	G SLEEVE LENGTH MEASURED FROM UNDERARM
XS	31" 79 cm	27.75" 70 cm	3.5" 9 cm	13" 33 cm	12" 30 cm	9.75" 25 cm	14" 36 cm
S	35" 89 cm	28.5" 72 cm	4" 10 cm	13" 33 cm	12.5" 32 cm	10.25" 26 cm	14" 36 cm
M	39" 99 cm	28.5" 72 cm	4" 10 cm	14" 36 cm	12.75" 32 cm	10.5" 27 cm	14" 36 cm
L	43" 109 cm	28.5" 72 cm	4.25" 11 cm	14" 36 cm	13.75" 35 cm	11.5" 29 cm	14" 36 cm
XL	47" 119 cm	29.25" 74 cm	4.25" 11 cm	15" 38 cm	15.25" 39 cm	13" 33 cm	14" 36 cm
2X	51" 130 cm	29.25" 74 cm	4.75" 12 cm	15" 38 cm	17.25" 44 cm	14" 36 cm	14" 36 cm
3X	55" 140 cm	29.25" 74 cm	4.75" 12 cm	15" 38 cm	18.75" 48 cm	15.5" 39 cm	14" 36 cm
4X	59" 150 cm	30" 76 cm	5" 13 cm	16" 41 cm	20.25" 51 cm	17" 43 cm	14" 36 cm
5X	63" 160 cm	30" 76 cm	5" 13 cm	16" 41 cm	20.25" 51 cm	17" 43 cm	14" 36 cm

This chart shows the finished garment measurements. This sweater is designed to be worn with approximately 1 to 3 inches (2.5 to 8 cm) of positive ease. Find the finished bust measurement in this chart and choose a size that is 1 to 3 inches (3 to 8 cm) larger than your actual bust measurement. For reference, the model is 5 feet, 4 inches (163 cm) tall with a 34-inch (86-cm) bust and is wearing a size small with a finished garment bust measurement of 35 inches (89 cm) with 1 inch (2.5 cm) of positive ease. If between sizes, size down.

For more information and tester photos, visit knitsnknots.ca/amber-magic.

BOR: beginning of round

ch: chain

csc: center single crochet (see Techniques Section on page 179)

csc2tog: center single crochet 2 stitches together

inc: increase—work 2 csc into designated stitch

PM: place marker

rep: repeat

rnd: round

sc: single crochet

sk: skip

sl st: slip stitch

st(s): stitch(es)

Schematic

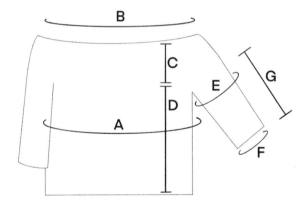

Amber Magic Pattern

Yoke

Ch 111 (114, 114, 114, 117) (117, 117, 120, 120), sl st into first ch to join rnd.

Rnd 1: Sc loosely in each ch to end of rnd. (The next rnd will be difficult to work if Rnd 1 is too tight!) [111 (114, 114, 114, 117) (117, 117, 120, 120) sc]

Work 1 csc straight into the first sc from Rnd 1 to set yourself up to work in a spiral. Place BOR marker in this csc.

> *Note:* Because you are working in a spiral, your BOR marker will gradually drift off-center. Simply replace it in the approximate center st as often as needed, using the tail from your beginning chain as a reference point.

Rnd 2: Csc in each sc to end of rnd.

> *Note:* The first few rounds are more difficult when it comes to finding the proper stitch placement. Once you have a few rounds worked, you will find your rhythm and it will become much easier!

Increase Rnd 1

*Inc in next st, csc in next 2 sts; rep from * to end of rnd. [148 (152, 152, 152, 156) (156, 156, 160, 160) csc]

Csc in each st for next 6 (6, 3, 3, 2) (2, 2, 2, 2) rnds.

Increase Rnd 2

XS: Csc in first 4 sts, *inc in next st, csc in next 5 sts; rep from * to end of rnd. [172 csc]

S: Inc in first st, csc in next 2 sts, *inc in next st, csc in next 3 sts; rep from * to last st, inc in last st. [191 csc]

All remaining sizes: *Inc in next st, sc in next 3 sts; rep from * to end of rnd. [x (x, 190, 190, 195) (195, 195, 200, 200) csc]

> *Customization Tip:* Refer to the yoke depth measurement in the Sizing Chart (page 152). You may want to try your sweater on periodically to see where the finished yoke would lie on your body. If it seems too deep for you (or not deep enough), you can eliminate non-increase rnds (or add more) before separating the yoke as you see fit.

Csc in each st for next 10 (13, 3, 3, 2) (2, 2, 2, 2) rnds.

Sizes XS and S finished with yoke; skip to Separating Body & Sleeves. All other sizes continue to Increase Rnd 3.

Increase Rnd 3

M: Csc in first 5 sts, *inc in next st, csc in next 8 sts; rep from * to last 5 sts, csc in last 5 sts. [210 csc]

L: Csc in first 5 sts, *inc in next st, csc in next 4 sts; rep from * to last 5 sts, csc in last 5 sts. [226 csc]

All remaining sizes: *Inc in next st, csc in next 4 sts; rep from * to end of rnd. [x (x, x, x, 234) (234, 234, 240, 240) csc]

Csc in each st for next x (x, 12, 14, 2) (2, 2, 2, 2) rnds.

Sizes M and L finished with yoke; skip to Separating Body & Sleeves. All other sizes continue to Increase Rnd 4.

3X: Inc in first st, csc in next 8 sts, *inc in next st, csc in next 10 sts; rep from * to end of rnd. [298 csc]

4X: Csc in first 14 sts, *inc in next st, csc in next 5 sts; rep from * to last 14 sts, csc in last 14 sts. [322 csc]

5X: *Inc in first st, csc in next 6 sts; rep from * to end of rnd. [320 csc]

Csc in each st for next x (x, x, x, x) (x, 12, 14, 2) rnds.

Sizes 3X and 4X finished with yoke; proceed to Separating Body & Sleeves. Size 5X continue to Increase Rnd 6.

Increase Rnd 6

5X: Csc in first 6 sts, *inc in next st, csc in next 21 sts; rep from * to last 6 sts, csc in last 6 sts. [334 csc]

5X only: Csc in each st for next 11 rnds.

All Sizes: At this point, your yoke should now have a total of 20 (23, 23, 25, 25) (27, 27, 29, 29) rnds completed.

Separating Body & Sleeves
Make sure your BOR marker is centered.

Csc in next 25 (29, 33, 36, 40) (43, 46, 50, 53) sts, ch 12 (12, 12, 14, 15) (16, 18, 19, 20), sk next 36 (38, 39, 41, 46) (53, 57, 62, 61) sts to create space for right sleeve, csc in next 50 (57, 66, 72, 79) (86, 92, 99, 106) sts, ch 12 (12, 12, 14, 15) (16, 18, 19, 20), sk next 36 (38, 39, 41, 46) (53, 57, 62, 61) sts to create space for left sleeve, csc in next 25 (29, 33, 36, 39) (43, 46, 49, 53) sts to BOR. [124 (139, 156, 172, 188) (204, 220, 236, 252) sts]

PM in first and last skipped st of each sleeve (2 markers per sleeve). You will need to refer to these markers when working the first sleeve round.

Increase Rnd 4

XL: Csc in first 5 sts, *inc in next st, csc in next 13 sts; rep from * to last 5 sts, csc in last 5 sts. [250 csc]

2X: Csc in first 7 sts, *inc in next st, csc in next 4 sts; rep from * to 7 sts remain, csc in last 7 sts. [278 csc]

3X, 4X and 5X: *Inc in next st, csc in next 5 sts; rep from * to end of rnd. [x (x, x, x, x) (x, 273, 280, 280) csc]

Csc in each st for next x (x, x, x, 13) (15, 2, 2, 2) rnds.

Size XL and 2X finished with yoke; skip to Separating Body & Sleeves. All other sizes continue to Increase Rnd 5.

Body

BOR marker can now be removed.

All sizes: Csc in each csc and each ch to end of rnd.

Csc in each st around until body measures 13 (13, 14, 14, 15) (15, 15, 16, 16)" (33 [33, 36, 36, 38] [38, 38, 41, 41] cm) from underarm or until desired length.

When satisfied with length, sl st into next 3 sts and fasten off.

Sleeves

Attach yarn with a sl st into the approximate center of the underarm with the right side facing you.

Rnd 1 (Set-Up Rnd): Work 6 (6, 6, 7, 7) (8, 9, 9, 10) csc evenly before first marker, csc in next 36 (38, 39, 41, 46) (53, 57, 62, 61) sleeve sts up to and including second marked st, work 6 (6, 6, 7, 8) (8, 9, 10, 10) csc evenly to end of rnd. [48 (50, 51, 55, 61) (69, 75, 81, 81) csc]

Csc directly into first csc from Set-Up Rnd to begin working in a spiral.

Place BOR marker into the approximate center st. Your marker will gradually drift off-center; simply replace it to the approximate center as often as needed, using the tail from where you attached your yarn as a reference point.

Rnds 2–5: Csc in all sts to end of rnd.

Rnd 6: Csc2tog, csc in all sts to end of rnd. [47 (49, 50, 54, 60) (68, 74, 80, 80) csc]

Rnds 7–11: Csc in all sts to end of rnd.

Rnd 12: Csc2tog, csc in all sts to end of rnd. [46 (48, 49, 53, 59) (67, 73, 79, 79) csc]

Work Rnds 7–12 another 4 (4, 4, 4, 4) (11, 11, 11, 11) times. [42 (44, 45, 49, 55) (56, 62, 68, 68) csc]

Next 27 (27, 27, 27, 27) (3, 3, 3, 3) rnds: Csc in each st around.

Size XS, S, M, L, XL only: Rep Rnds 6–11 three more times. [39 (41, 42, 46, 52) (x, x, x, x) csc]

Customization Tip: The sleeves of this sweater are designed to be three-quarter-length. For full-length sleeves, continue working csc in all sts until desired sleeve length. You may choose to continue your decrease pattern (decreasing every sixth row or so) to create a fitted wrist. Try your sweater on as you work your sleeves to ensure you achieve your desired circumference and length. Keep note of any alterations you make to your first sleeve so that you can easily alter the second sleeve to match.

All sizes: Once satisfied with the sleeve length, sl st into next 3 sts, fasten off.

Rep all instructions for the second sleeve.

Weave in any remaining ends and block your sweater to the dimensions listed in the Sizing Chart (page 152).

Garnet Bay
Cold-Shoulder

This style of sweater is called a "cold-shoulder" sweater for obvious reasons, and the tastefully exposed shoulders lend a modern, edgy look. The wide, feminine sleeves land just before the wrist and become more tapered as you move up the arm, artfully drawing your eyes up to the cheeky, exposed shoulder. This design experiments with negative space, accentuating the exposed area where the sweater doesn't exist.

The height of the front and back necklines can be adjusted to suit your exact taste—whether you prefer a high neck or low neck. Can't choose? Make both! This sweater is reversible, so you can work the front and back to different heights and wear either side as the front for two distinct looks. Garnet Bay can be a charming holiday sweater, or a breezy summer top, or omit the sleeves completely for a cute tank top.

Construction

The body of this sweater is worked from the bottom up in seamless, joined rounds. The body is then split to work a front and back section, which are later connected with narrow straps. The sleeves are worked separately from the bottom up and then joined to the body at the underarm. Last, a few finishing rounds are worked to smooth out the shoulder cutouts.

Materials

Yarn:
Sport—Premier Cotton Fair in Succulent (52% cotton, 48% acrylic)
317 yds (290 m) per 3.5-oz (100-g) ball
Find this yarn on premieryarns.com or visit yarnsub.com to find comparable substitutes.

Yardage:
5 (6, 6, 7, 7) (7, 8, 8, 9) balls or 1450 (1600, 1700, 1900, 2025) (2150, 2325, 2425, 2575) yds [1326 (1464, 1555, 1738, 1852) (1966, 2126, 2218, 2355) m]

Note: Budget friendly!
Substitute Premier Cotton Fair with any similar sport weight, category #2 yarn that matches gauge. You do not necessarily have to use a cotton yarn for this pattern to work; most fibers will produce a beautiful sweater.

Hook:
Size U.S. E/4 (3.5 mm) or size needed to obtain gauge

Notions:
Tapestry needle, locking stitch markers

Gauge:
4 x 4" (10 x 10 cm) = 18.5 sts and 18 rows in stitch pattern (see instructions below)
Ch 22.

Row 1: Sc in 2nd ch from hook, *dc in next ch, sc in next ch; rep from * to end of row, turn.

Row 2: Ch 1, sc in first sc, *dc in next dc, sc in next sc; rep from * to end of row, turn.

Rep Row 2 until you have at least 22 rows completed.

Block your swatch. Measure the inner 4 inches (10 cm) of your blocked swatch to get the most accurate measurement.

ABBREVIATIONS
Written in U.S. crochet terms
BOR: beginning of round
ch(s): chain(s)
dc: double crochet
FSC: foundation single crochet (see
Foundation Stitches in the Techniques
section on page 172)
PM: place marker
rep: repeat
rnd: round
sc: single crochet
sc2tog: single crochet 2 stitches together
sk: skip
sl st: slip stitch
st(s): stitch(es)
work in patt: work in pattern—this means
to sc in each sc and dc in each dc

Schematic

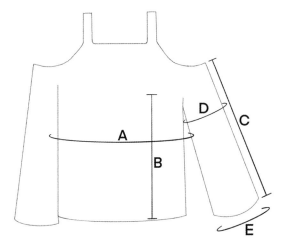

Garnet Bay Sizing Chart

	A FINISHED BUST CIRCUMFERENCE	B BODY LENGTH MEASURED FROM UNDERARM	C SLEEVE LENGTH MEASURED FROM UNDERARM	D UPPER ARM CIRCUMFERENCE	E WRIST CIRCUMFERENCE
XS	29" 74 cm	17" 43 cm	16" 41 cm	9.75" 25 cm	16.25" 41 cm
S	33.5" 85 cm	17" 43 cm	16" 41 cm	10" 25.5 cm	16.25" 41 cm
M	37" 94 cm	17" 43 cm	16" 41 cm	11" 28 cm	16.25" 41 cm
L	41" 104 cm	17" 43 cm	16" 41 cm	12" 30 cm	16.75" 42.5 cm
XL	45.5" 116 cm	17" 43 cm	16" 41 cm	13.5" 34 cm	16.75" 42.5 cm
2X	49" 124 cm	17" 43 cm	16" 41 cm	15.25" 39 cm	17" 43 cm
3X	53.5" 136 cm	17" 43 cm	16" 41 cm	17" 43 cm	17" 43 cm
4X	56.5" 144 cm	17" 43 cm	16" 41 cm	18.5" 47 cm	17.5" 44 cm
5X	61" 155 cm	17" 43 cm	16" 41 cm	18.5" 47 cm	17.5" 44 cm

This chart shows the finished garment measurements. This sweater is designed to be fitted, worn with up to 1 inch (2.5 cm) of positive or negative ease. When choosing a size, find the bust measurement in this chart that is closest to your actual bust measurement and make this size. For example, the model is 5 feet, 4 inches (163 cm) tall with a 34-inch (86-cm) bust and is wearing a size small with a finished garment bust measurement of 33 inches (84 cm), worn with 1 inch (2.5 cm) of negative ease. If between sizes, size down.

For more information and tester photos, visit knitsnknots.ca/garnet-bay.

Garnet Bay Pattern

Body

Rnd 1: FSC 135 (155, 171, 191, 211) (227, 247, 263, 283), sl st into first st to join rnd, turn.

> *Note:* The body of this sweater (as well as each sleeve) is worked in joined, turned rounds. Make sure to slip stitch into the first stitch of the row to join your round, and then turn your work to begin your next round in the opposite direction.

Rnd 2: Ch 1, sc in first st, *dc in next st, sc in next st; rep from * to end of row, sl st into first sc to join rnd, turn. [135 (155, 171, 191, 211) (227, 247, 263, 283) sts]

Rnd 3: Ch 1, sc in first sc, *dc in next dc, sc in next sc; rep from * to end of row, sl st into first sc to join rnd, turn.

Rep Rnd 3 until you have worked a total of 77 rnds or until you reach the desired length from underarm. Hold your sample up to your underarms, and when you are satisfied with length, proceed.

You will now separate the work into two sections: Front and Back.

Front

Row 1: Ch 1, sl st across first 10 (12, 14, 16, 16) (18, 20, 20, 20) sts, ch 1, sc in next st, PM in this sc to mark new BOR, *dc in next st, sc in next st; rep from * 22 (25, 27, 30, 35) (37, 40, 44, 49) more times, stop here, count 19 (23, 29, 31, 33) (37, 39, 41, 41) sts and place a marker in last counted st which should be a dc (you will come back to this when you work the Back section), turn. [47 (53, 57, 63, 73) (77, 83, 91, 101) sts]

Row 2: Ch 1, sk first sc, dc in next dc, *sc in next sc, dc in next dc; rep from * until 1 sc remains, sk last sc, turn. [decreases row by 2 sts]

Row 3: Ch 1, sk first dc, sc in next sc, *dc in next dc, sc in next sc; rep from * until 1 dc remains, sk last dc, turn. [decreases row by 2 sts]

Rep Rows 2 and 3 until you reach your desired coverage, then fasten off. You can work to any height you like as you will be working the straps using your specific measurements based on the height of your front and back panels here.

Back

Insert hook with new yarn into marked dc, and join with a sl st. The first sc of Row 1 will be worked into the sc after the sl st.

Row 1: Ch 1, sc in next sc, *dc in next dc, sc in next sc; rep from * 23 (26, 27, 31, 34) (37, 42, 44, 48) more times, turn. [49 (55, 57, 65, 71) (77, 87, 91, 99) sts]

Row 2: Ch 1, sk first sc, dc in next dc, *sc in next sc, dc in next dc; rep from * until 1 sc remains, sk last sc, turn. [decreases row by 2 sts]

Row 3: Ch 1, sk first dc, sc in next sc, *dc in next dc, sc in next sc; rep from * until 1 dc remains, sk last dc, turn. [decreases row by 2 sts]

Rep Rows 2 and 3 until you reach your desired coverage, do not fasten off; you will continue with this yarn when you work the first strap. You can work to any height you like as you will be working the straps using your specific measurements based on the height of your front and back panels here.

> *Customization Tip:* Because this sweater is reversible, you can work the back of your sweater to a different height than the front to have two different neckline options.

Try your sweater on to figure out how long you would like your straps to be to connect your front and back sections. Make note of this length. Keep in mind that your straps may stretch with wear, so it's best to work them slightly shorter than your desired length.

Straps

Note: The straps are worked by trying on the sweater and working a chain that equals your desired strap length, because the front and back sections are worked until your desired height. This gives you a lot of space to be creative and really customize this top to fit your body the way you like. So, when you get to the straps, don't overthink this—just work any chain length that gives you a strap that you are comfortable with. Then, when you work over this chain in the stitch pattern, it does not matter whether your row ends with a single crochet or a double crochet, just follow the stitch pattern you have established for yourself.

Continuing with same yarn, work a ch that measures your desired strap length, sl st into corresponding st on top edge of front panel to join Back Panel to Front Panel. It does not matter if you have an even or odd number of chs, just take note of how many you worked so you can make an identical strap on the other side. Sl st into next st along top row of the front, turn to work back on ch just created.

Row 1: Sk sl sts, sc into first ch, *dc into next ch, sc into next ch; rep from * across ch, note that you may not complete the last full st repeat, sl st into next 2 sts along top row of back, turn to work back on row just worked.

Row 2: Sk sl sts, work in patt across strap, sl st into next 2 sts along top row of panel, turn to work back on row just worked.

Rows 3–5: Rep Row 2 for 3 more rows, or until strap is 1 inch (2.5 cm) less than your desired strap width.

Note that another 1 inch (2.5 cm) or so will be worked on the other side of the initial chain from the strap after sleeves are attached, so the strap at this point is approximately 1 inch (2.5 cm) less than the final width.

Fasten off.

For the second strap, attach yarn to the opposite corner st on either the front or back panel, and rep all instructions for the first strap.

Sleeves (Make 2)

The sleeves are worked from the bottom up, starting at the widest points, decreasing toward the elbow, then increasing toward the upper arm.

When instructed to increase, work the rnd as follows: Ch 1, work 2 sts in first st, maintaining st pattern, continue to work in patt to end of rnd, work 1 more st into last st while maintaining st pattern, sl st to join, turn. [Increases rnd by 2 sts]

Note on Increase Rnds: When adding a st to the beginning of the rnd, look at the first st in the row below. If this first st is a sc, your new rnd will begin like this: Ch 1, (dc, sc) in first sc, dc in next dc, sc in next sc, etc. If the first st is a dc, your new rnd will begin like this: Ch 1, (sc, dc) in first dc, sc in next sc, dc in next dc, etc. This way, you will not interfere with your previously established stitch pattern, you will simply add to it.

Every rnd that is not an increase rnd or decrease rnd is worked as follows: Ch 1, work in patt to end of rnd, sl st to join, turn.

Follow your size only; total number of rnds given includes the 2 rnds you just completed.

Decreases

Work each rnd in patt, decreasing in Rnd 16 and then in every even numbered rnd until you have completed Rnd 44 (42, 38, 42, 40) (38, 38, 40, 40), then work each rnd in patt until you have completed Rnd 72 (72, 72, 51, 41) (39, 39, 41, 41). [45 (47, 51, 49, 51) (55, 55, 55, 55) sts]

Rnd 1: FSC 75 (75, 75, 77, 77) (79, 79, 81, 81), sl st into first st to join rnd, turn.

Rnd 2: Ch 1, sc in first st, *dc in next st, sc in next st; rep from * to end of rnd, sl st to join, turn. [75 (75, 75, 77, 77) (79, 79, 81, 81) sts]

For the remainder of the sleeve, work the rnds as specified for your size below:

When instructed to decrease, work the rnd as follows: Ch 1, sk first st, work in patt until 1 st remains unworked, sk last st, sl st into first st to join, turn. [Decreases rnd by 2 sts]

Sizes XS, S, and M have completed the sleeve—for longer sleeve (sizes XS, S, M only), rep last rnd until desired length. Fasten off, leaving a 12-inch (30-cm) tail for attaching the sleeve to the body.

All remaining sizes: Proceed to Increases.

Increases

Continue working each rnd in patt, increasing in Rnd x (x, x, 52, 42) (40, 40, 42, 42) and then in every even numbered rnd until you have completed Rnd x (x, x, 56, 52) (54, 62, 68, 68), then work each rnd in patt until you have completed Rnd 72. [x (x, x, 55, 63) (71, 79, 83, 83) sts]

For a longer sleeve, rep last rnd until you reach the desired length. The sleeve is now complete for all sizes. Fasten off, leaving a 12-inch (30-cm) tail for attaching the sleeve to the body.

Attaching Sleeves

Place the sleeves at each underarm, centering the sleeve seams along the underarm space on the body using locking stitch markers to hold the sleeves in place. With your 12-inch (30-cm) tail and a tapestry needle, seam along the underarm so that approximately 4 to 5 inches (10 to 13 cm) of sleeve gets seamed to the body. Try your sweater on and adjust if necessary.

Cold-Shoulder Finishing Rounds

Next, you will stitch along the opening of each "cold-shoulder" space, connecting the sleeve and body. This will help connect the sleeves to the sweater for a more cohesive look. You will place a few decreases on either side of each sleeve where the sleeve joins the body. As you work around this shoulder opening, there are no obvious places to work your stitches, so simply place them wherever looks right to you. Note that it will be better to have fewer sts here than too many because you want these finishing rnds to tighten and conform to your body and not be too loose.

Attach new yarn with a sl st where the sleeve meets the body so that you can work across the sleeve first.

Rnd 1: Ch 1, work in patt across sleeve until reaching the opposite sleeve–body join, then cont in patt along body, across strap, then down other side of body, and back to your starting point, sl st into first st to join in the rnd, turn.

Rnd 2: Ch 1, sk first st, work in patt around until you have completed a dc just before the opposite sleeve–body join, sc2tog working the next 2 sc together, skipping over 1 dc in between them, then cont in patt to end of rnd, turn.

Rep Rnd 2 two more times. Try on your sweater. If you want this shoulder cutout to be smaller or tighter, work additional rnds, decreasing where you see fit. For these finishing rnds, it is not important that you stay in perfect st pattern, so you can decrease however you like. You can also try working this part in a smaller hook to get a tighter fit.

Rep for the second side.

Weave in any remaining ends and block your sweater to the dimensions listed in the Sizing Chart (page 161).

A Beginner's Guide to Reading Patterns

Reading a pattern with instructions for nine sizes can take some getting used to. At first glance, the numbers may seem overwhelming, but remember that when you take into account the numbers that apply to your size, the instructions are actually quite basic. You may want to circle the numbers that pertain to your size before beginning. Or, if you don't want to write in this book, you can take a picture of the pattern and digitize it or print it out to write on.

Each of the patterns has nine sizes ranging from XS to 5X except for a few oversized designs that have merged two or three sizes together while maintaining the same size range. Sizes are written as follows: XS (S, M, L, XL) (2X, 3X, 4X, 5X). When working the pattern, you will only follow the numbers that pertain to your size. For example:

Sc in the next 3 (4, 5, 6, 7) (8, 9, 10, 11) sts.

This set of instructions means size XS will single crochet in the next 3 stitches, size L will single crochet in the next 6 stitches and size 5X will single crochet in the next 11 stitches. Two sets of parentheses are included to make it easier to find your size because it can look a bit jumbled when eight different numbers are written inside one set of parentheses. The number before the parentheses is the value for size XS, the first set of parentheses contain sizes S through XL, and the second set of parentheses contains sizes 2X through 5X. Once you know the placement of your size, it will become second nature to follow the numbers written just for you.

If only one value is provided, it applies to all sizes. For example:

Hdc in each st around for the next 4 rows.

This means that all sizes are instructed to half double crochet each stitch around for the next 4 rows.

Sometimes you are instructed to work until a specified measurement, rather than work a specified number of rows. Imperial and metric will always be provided, with imperial written first, followed by the corresponding metric units. For example:

Hdc in each st until work measures 12 inches (30 cm).

This means to work one half double crochet into each stitch until your work measures 12 inches (or 30 cm if you follow the metric units).

Symbols Used

[ ]—Repeat the sequence inside the brackets as many times as indicated immediately following the brackets.
Example: [dc in next st, sc in next st] 6 (6, 6, 6, 7) (7, 8, 8, 8) times.

( )—Work the sequence inside the parentheses into the same stitch/space.
Example: (sc, ch 2, dc) in next ch-sp.

*—Indicates the beginning of a sequence that is to be repeated as many times as indicated.
Example 1: Ch 1, sc in first sc, *ch 1, sk next ch-sp, sc in next sc; rep from * to end of row, turn.
Example 2: Ch 1, sc in next st, *dc in next st, sc in next st; rep from * 23 (26, 27, 31, 34) (37, 42, 44, 48) more times, turn.

* instructions within asterisks *—Indicates to repeat the sequence in between the asterisks as many times as indicated.
Example: Ch 1, sc in first sc, *ch 1, sk next ch-sp, sc in next sc*; rep from * to * across Side 1 until 1 ch-sp and 1 sc remain unworked.

Techniques

Seaming

Most of the patterns in this book have a little bit of seaming, whether it's attaching all the panels or seaming just the sleeve cuffs. My go-to seaming method is the whip stitch, though you are more than welcome to use any seaming method you like for any of the patterns in the book. Whip stitch is just what I find easiest and is unnoticeable in most cases.

Whip Stitch

Step 1—Insert your threaded tapestry needle through corresponding stitches on both panels. Tighten.

Step 2—Next, insert the needle into the next set of corresponding stitches from the same direction as Step 1.

Step 3—Repeat Step 2 until seaming is complete.

Crocheting Evenly Around a Neckline

In some patterns, you will be instructed to work evenly around a neckline. Usually, there will not be obvious or distinct stitch placements for you to work into. Working a neckline is intuitive, and you have the freedom to place stitches however you see fit. Use your judgment to achieve your desired look. This step is usually used as a set-up round before working neckline ribbing, and other times it is used as a finishing row to clean up any raw edges.

Working into the Edge (or Row-Ends) of Established Ribbing, Hem or Sleeve Cuff

Most of the bottom-up projects in this book begin with the bottom hem (usually ribbing) of one panel, establishing the width of the garment. The next step is to begin the body of the fabric by working into the row-ends of this established ribbing to work across the width of the garment. This creates a row that is perpendicular to the ribbing. (This technique applies to bottom-up sleeves that begin at the wrist cuff, too.)

To work into the row-ends of a bottom hem or ribbing, you will be instructed to turn your work to set yourself up to work across the length of your ribbing, stitching into the ends of the rows you just completed.

To work across single crochet, back loops only (scBLO) ribbing, you will be instructed to work 1 single crochet into the ends of each row you just completed.

There is not an exact place for your stitch to go when working into the row-ends, so place your hook into the end of the row wherever looks right. Continue across the entire width of the ribbing. You should finish this row with the same number of stitches as there are rows. If you had 50 rows of ribbing, you should finish with 50 single crochet stitches after working 1 stitch into each row-end.

To work across hdc bottom hem, you will be instructed to work 3 hdc for every 2 rows in the bottom hem. This is because hdc stitches are taller than they are wide, and the height of 2 stitches equals the width of 3 stitches. Like working into the edge of any type of crochet fabric, there are no distinct placements for your hook to go; this is more intuitive, so place them as evenly as you can. The important thing is that you end up with the proper stitch count.

I like to use stitch markers to help keep track of my stitch count and make sure it corresponds with how many rows of hem I have worked into. When you've made your way across part of the row, double-check that your count is on track and place a marker so you know that everything is correct up to this point.

After 2 rows of hem, you should have worked 3 hdc. After 4 rows of hem, you should have worked 6 hdc. After 10 rows of hem, you should have worked 15 hdc, and so on.

Yarn-Over Slip Stitch Ribbing (yo-slst)

This ribbing technique is used in the Fifty Below Color Block Pullover (page 62). This stitch is worked into the third loop for most of the ribbing and is worked underneath the front and back loops like a regular stitch at the beginning and end of the ribbing rows.

Step 1a—Work a chain, here work 11.

Step 2a—Yarn over, insert hook into 2nd chain from hook.

Step 3a—Yarn over, draw loop through stitch.

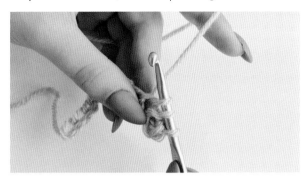

Step 4a—Draw yarn immediately through both loops on hook (first yo-slst completed).

To complete the rest of the row:

Step 1b—Yarn over, insert hook into next stitch, yarn over.

Step 2b—Draw yarn immediately through both loops on hook.

Repeat Steps 1b and 2b to the end of the row, then turn to begin working back on this row.

To complete all remaining rows:

Step 1c—Chain 1, yarn over, insert hook through both loops of first stitch, draw yarn through stitch and immediately through all loops on hook.

Step 2c—Yarn over, insert hook into 3rd loop of next stitch (the loop that appears in the very front of your work), draw yarn through stitch and immediately through all loops on hook.

Step 3c—Repeat Step 2c across row until 1 stitch remains unworked.

Step 4c—Yarn over, insert hook through both loops of stitch, draw yarn through stitch and immediately through all loops on hook, just like you did in Step 1c of this row. Turn.

Repeat Steps 1c–4c until you reach the desired amount of ribbing.

Applied Ribbing

This technique is a way to add ribbing to an existing fabric and is used in many of the patterns in this book to create sleeve cuffs, ribbed bottom hems and ribbed necklines.

Step 1—Work a chain. This will be specified in the pattern. In this example, work 10 chains.

Step 2—Turn to work back on this chain you just created, single crochet in 2nd chain from hook and in each chain across. You will finish this step with 9 single crochet stitches. Each remaining row will contain 9 stitches.

Step 3—To attach this protruding row of stitches, slip stitch into the next 2 stitches from the base on which you are working. If you are working an applied sleeve cuff, you will slip stitch into the next 2 stitches from your last sleeve round. This attaches your new work to your existing work. (Photo shows 2 slip stitches created.)

Count your stitches to make sure you still have the correct number without accidentally adding or eliminating any.

Step 4—Turn work to begin crocheting back on your new row, skip over the 2 slip stitches just created and single crochet into the first single crochet from your new ribbing row through the back loops only (BLO). Continue to single crochet (BLO) into each single crochet stitch until reaching the end of the row. Sometimes, you will be instructed to work this last stitch through both loops like a normal single crochet stitch rather than just the back loop to produce a cleaner edge, other times you will be instructed to continue working through the back loops only to produce a ribbing with more stretch.

Repeat Steps 2–4 until you reach the desired amount of ribbing. Note that Step 2 refers to working into a chain rather than a row of single crochets. However, once you are repeating this sequence, you will be working into single crochets instead of chains.

How to Weave in Ends

This isn't usually a technique included in how-to sections, but it's a question I get a lot. Just in case you're curious, here's how I do it:

First and foremost, you want your ends to be secure, but you also want to make sure the yarn remains hidden.

After you finish the stitchwork and fasten off, tie a double knot with the tail into a nearby stitch.

To avoid having the tail end pop out the right side of your sweater, use the needle to separate the plies of the yarn and weave each ply of the tail through only a few plies on the wrong side of your fabric so that the tail end is certain to remain on the inside of your sweater. Make sure to weave the yarn through a few different directions. Snip yarn and gently stretch the fabric in all directions to hide the tail.

To weave in ends in a section of ribbing, tie a double knot and use your tapestry needle to weave the tail end around the stitches until reaching the fabric above the ribbing. Weave the tail end through approximately half the plies of yarn on the inside of your garment. Snip yarn and gently stretch the fabric in all directions to hide the tail.

Foundation Stitches

An important skill for every crocheter to master, foundation stitches are used in most patterns throughout this book. Foundation stitches allow a crocheter to combine an initial chain with the first row of a project to produce a stretch similar to regular stitches instead of beginning with a normal chain, which is rigid and has much less stretch than all other stitches.

Foundation Single Crochet (FSC)
Step 1a—Chain 2.

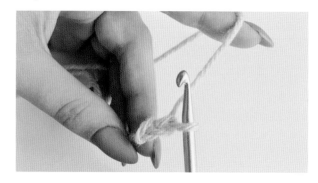

Step 2a—Insert hook into second chain from hook, yarn over.

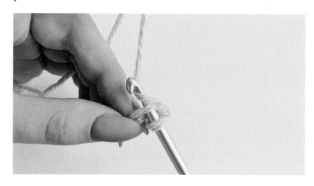

Step 3a—Draw yarn through stitch (2 loops on hook).

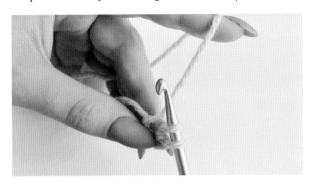

Step 4a—Yarn over, draw yarn through 1 loop on hook (this creates the first chain—the first half of the FSC).

Step 5a—Yarn over, draw yarn through remaining 2 loops on hook (this creates the single crochet—the second half of the FSC). One FSC is completed at this point.

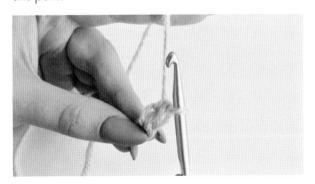

To create the next FSC stitch:

Step 1b—Insert hook under the 2 loops of the chain at the bottom of the previous FSC.

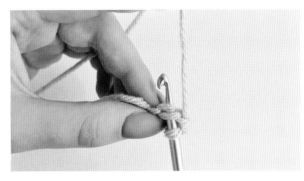

Step 2b—Yarn over and draw yarn through stitch (2 loops on hook).

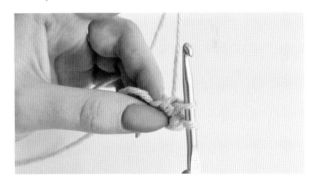

Step 3b—Yarn over and draw yarn through 1 loop (this creates the chain).

Step 4b—Yarn over and draw yarn through 2 loops (this creates the single crochet).

Repeat Steps 1b–4b as many times as pattern indicates.

Foundation Half Double Crochet (FHDC)
Step 1a—Chain 2.

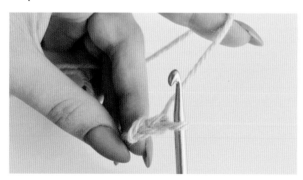

Step 2a—Yarn over, insert hook into second chain from hook.

Step 3a—Yarn over, draw yarn through stitch (3 loops on hook).

Step 4a—Yarn over and draw yarn through 1 loop (this creates the chain portion of the FHDC).

Step 5a—Yarn over and draw through 3 loops (this creates the half double crochet half of a FHDC). At this point, one FHDC is complete.

To create the next FHDC stitch:

Step 1b—Yarn over, insert hook under 2 loops of chain at the bottom of the previous FHDC.

Step 2b—Yarn over and draw yarn through stitch (3 loops on hook).

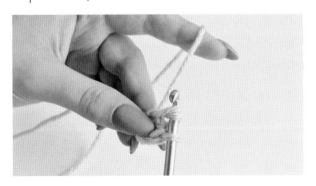

Step 3b—Yarn over and draw yarn through 1 loop (creating 1 chain).

Step 4b—Yarn over and draw yarn through 3 loops (creating 1 half double crochet).

Repeat Steps 1b–4b as many times as pattern indicates.

Foundation Double Crochet (FDC)

Step 1a—Chain 3.

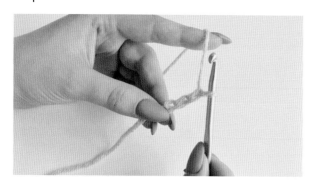

Step 2a—Yarn over, insert hook into third chain from hook.

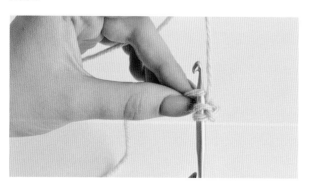

Step 3a—Yarn over, draw yarn through stitch (3 loops on hook).

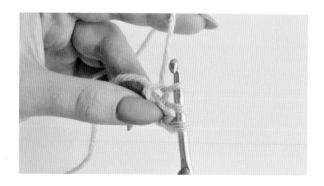

Step 4a—Yarn over, draw yarn through 1 loop (this creates 1 chain).

Step 5a—Yarn over, draw yarn through 2 loops (this creates part of the first double crochet).

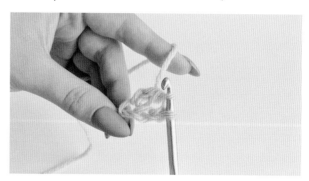

Step 6a—Yarn over, draw yarn through 2 loops (this completes the first double crochet). At this point, one FDC is complete.

To create the next FDC stitch:

Step 1b—Yarn over, insert hook under 2 loops of chain at the bottom of the previous FDC.

Step 2b—Yarn over and draw yarn through stitch (3 loops on hook).

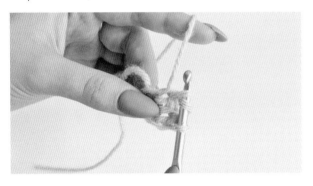

Step 3b—Yarn over and draw yarn through 1 loop (this creates a chain).

Step 4b—Yarn over and draw yarn through 2 loops on hook. (This is the first part of the double crochet.)

Step 5b—Yarn over and draw yarn through 2 loops on hook. (This completes the double crochet component of the FDC.)

Repeat Steps 1b–5b as many times as pattern indicates.

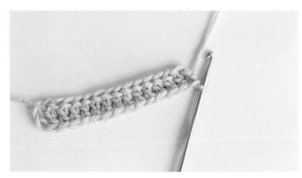

How to Seamlessly Change Colors

When working the last stitch of an old color, work the stitch as usual, but use the new color to do your final yarn-over and pull through to close the stitch. Then, you may cut the old color and continue stitching with the new color. In this example, you will be using the double crochet stitch. In this book, color changes only happen when beginning a new row; however, you may use this technique any time you want to change a color at any point in a pattern. If working in joined rounds, treat color changes in the same way: Work the last yarn-over and pull through the final stitch of the round in the new color, then work the slip stitch join and turning chain in the new color. Cut the old color, and continue working with the new color.

Seaming Pockets onto a Garment

Before attaching a pocket, make sure it is placed exactly where you want it. You may want to use stitch markers to help keep it perfectly square to your project while you seam. Always attach the pocket slightly higher than your desired placement to compensate for growth of your fabric that occurs over time through wear, and especially if your chosen fiber tends to grow upon blocking or washing.

While seaming around the perimeter of your pocket:

Step 1—Insert threaded tapestry needle from the right side through both layers of fabric, finishing on the inside of your work.

Step 2—Insert needle from the wrong side through both layers of fabric, finishing on the right side of your work.

Repeat Steps 1 and 2 until pocket is seamed.

Center Single Crochet Stitch

The center single crochet stitch is worked the same way as a regular single crochet stitch—the only difference is the placement of your hook. Insert your hook in between the two posts of the single crochet stitch, rather than underneath the front and back loops of the stitch. This stitch placement creates the appearance of stacked Vs, similar to the look of knitting.

If you're having trouble, try pulling your loop up a little higher than you normally would before working your final yarn-over to make it a little easier for you to work into this stitch on the following round.

Working Sleeves on a Top-Down Yoke

A few patterns in this book are worked from the top down with raglan or circular yoke shaping. These patterns are unique in that they create a garment by simultaneously constructing the sleeves and body panels while working from the neck toward the underarms. Next, the yoke is divided to separate the sleeves from the body. The body is worked next, and the sleeves are worked last. When working the sleeves, these patterns will always set you up to place stitch markers in your first and last sleeve stitch to distinguish which stitches come from the yoke, and which stitches need to be added to account for the space created from the underarm chains. This makes it easy to establish the first round of the sleeve. After completing the first round, the remainder of the sleeve is relatively straightforward.

Step 1—Attach yarn in the approximate center of underarm.

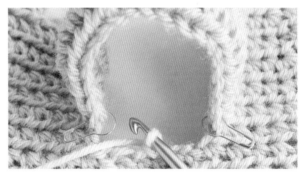

Step 2—Work a specified number of stitches before first marker.

Step 3—Work into the first marked stitch, then work into every sleeve stitch up to and including second marker.

Step 4—Work a specified number of stitches to end of rnd.

Step 5—At this point, the pattern will either indicate to join with a slip stitch into the first stitch of the round, or to work directly into the first stitch of the round to set yourself up to work in a spiral.

Bow

To create the bow in the back of the Burning Embers V-Neck (page 119):

Fold the rectangle in half, aligning the first and last row.

Seam the three open edges of the rectangle closed with a tapestry needle using the tail ends (the rectangle should feel a bit stiff and structured).

Work the smaller rectangle, finishing the edge as shown.

Use the smaller rectangle to wrap the larger rectangle, pinching it in the center.

Use a tapestry needle to secure the smaller rectangle in place.

Seam the bow to the sweater on the back side of the bow to best hide the seam.

Blocking

Blocking is the process of using water to relax your stitches, fix any curling edges and achieve the proper garment measurements. Blocking knitwear is like ironing wrinkly fabric. It is the final step of crocheting a sweater. Just as you would iron a wrinkly shirt so that it can be worn and presented in the best way, you block knitwear. You are essentially making your stitches neater, allowing the fibers of your yarn to relax and shaping your garment to achieve the intended measurements. This fixes any curled edges or wonky stitches and flattens the fabric out to create a neat, more polished garment. There are a few ways to block your knitwear:

Steam—You can pin your garment to a blocking board to the correct dimensions, and then use a hand steamer to gently relax the stitches. Let the work dry completely before removing it from the blocking board.

Wet Block—Soak your finished garment in lukewarm water with a bit of mild detergent. Use a towel to gently squeeze out any excess water, then lay it flat to dry. A laundry drying rack can be useful because air can flow above and below your drying garment, or you can let it dry on any flat surface or use T-pins on a blocking board to help your work keep its shape.

Spray—Pin your finished work on a blocking board to the correct dimensions, then spray your finished garment with water. Let your work dry completely before removing it from the blocking board.

Let your garments dry away from direct sunlight (this can fade the color of certain yarns) and use a fan to help speed up the process if desired.

Taking Care of Your Finished Sweaters

Most handmade knitwear requires similar care: Handwash in lukewarm water with wool wash or mild detergent, then press with or roll in a towel to remove the excess water and lay flat to dry.

Some yarns are machine washable and dryable including acrylic, most cottons and superwash yarns. Always check the label on your yarn for specific care instructions before machine washing or drying to avoid felting.

Store your finished sweaters by folding, never on a hanger. Over time, gravity will stretch your sweaters and can permanently ruin the shape of your sweaters if they are hung on hangers. (I have ruined a few knit and crochet sweaters from doing this, and they are misshapen beyond repair—even washing and blocking will not fix them!)

Resources

Craft Yarn Council: https://www.craftyarncouncil.com

Sizing info: https://www.craftyarncouncil.com/standards/woman-size

Knits 'N Knots Supplementary Content: https://knitsnknots.ca/book

More Knits 'N Knots Patterns on Ravelry: https://www.ravelry.com/people/KnitsNKnotsWpg

More Knits 'N Knots Patterns on My Website: https://www.knitsnknots.shop/

Lion Brand Yarn: https://www.lionbrand.com/

Yarnspirations: https://www.yarnspirations.com/

WeCrochet: https://www.crochet.com/

Premier: https://www.premieryarns.com/

In addition to the links above, Knits 'N Knots patterns can also be found on Etsy, crochet.com, lovecrafts.com and lionbrand.com under the same name.

Acknowledgments

Mom

Thank you for everything. Thank you for letting me turn your basement into my own personal yarn store in the early days. One of my favorite memories was making loom hats and drinking wine together while we prepared for market season. You always believe in me. Even when I told you I was going to drop my master's program to pursue knitting and crochet, you never doubted me for a second, and that means more to me than you will ever know. You give me unconditional love and support, and that's all I could ever ask for in a parent. You are more than just a mom to me, you are a friend. I love you so much.

Dad

Thank you for your unwavering support throughout my whole life. You taught me to follow my heart and give everything my best effort. I am so lucky to have had such an encouraging, gentle, loving father. I spend every day trying to be more like you. Growing up, I watched you excel at whatever you tried because of your determination to find creative solutions to any problem, and I like to think a bit of that rubbed off on me. I wish the crochet part of my life overlapped with our time together. There are so many reasons I am grateful to you, but most of all for loving your family so fiercely. I miss you every day and I wish I could share this book with you.

Laura

Hey sis. I like the dynamic we've built over the years, consisting of you calling me a grandma, and me making fun of your overuse of glitter. You are somehow a perfect balance of toughness and sparkle, and I wouldn't change a thing about you. Thank you for helping me out on market weekends when I know you probably had a million things you'd have rather been doing than sitting at my booth with me for 8+ hours. I love that we were able to bond over craft shows, and even do them together at our own booths. You are so much cooler than I like to admit, and I'm so happy to call you my sister and friend.

Matt

Oh Matt… Where to begin? When I think back on this writing process, my fondest memories are sitting in my office at the beautiful desk that you built for me, eating a meal you cooked for me, drinking a beer you brought to me. Thank you for showing me what it's like to selflessly, wholeheartedly support somebody, and for being my personal chef, my business partner, my quarantine buddy, my best friend. I am so grateful for everything you did for me so that I could cross "author" off my bucket list. Becoming an author is something I am so proud of, but being loved by you will always be my greatest honor. We make the best team and there is nothing we can't accomplish together.

Emily Reiter

Emily, your attention to detail has given me the confidence to share my patterns knowing they have been thoroughly reviewed by a true perfectionist. Your ability to examine somebody else's pattern with a fine-tooth comb and catch even the most minor errors is what makes you truly invaluable to this book. Thank you for being such a gifted proofreader, my second set of eyes in the early stages of this manuscript and for graciously suggesting ways to enhance the pattern-following experience, allowing crocheters to seamlessly read and execute these patterns with confidence and certainty. I am so grateful for the working relationship we've built over the last few years. I'm sure you won't miss checking your computer on a Monday morning to see that I've sent you ten separate emails. Thank you for taking on this book with me and helping me make it so, so, so much better.

Stephanie

To one of the most talented people I have ever met, this book would not be what it is without you. The first time I saw your photos I knew I had to work with you someday. You already know how obsessed I am with your work—there is something so unique about your editing style that I just can't get enough of.

The pieces in this book are so close to my heart, and it makes me unbelievably proud to flip through these pages and see these images. You are a true artist. I had so much fun working on this book with you, and I can't wait to see what other art we create together. I used to call you my photographer, now I call you my friend. Thank you for presenting my work in such a remarkable way. Love, your biggest fan.

Page Street Publishing

I've only been crocheting for 5 years, but all my life I've wanted to write a book. I am forever grateful to Page Street Publishing for taking a chance on me and allowing me to add "author" to my résumé. Most importantly, I am thankful for being given the freedom to create the book I wanted to create. I always wondered what a publisher–author relationship was like, and this was so much better than I expected. Emily was so helpful in answering my questions along the way and made this such a smooth, enjoyable process for me. Thank you for playing a special part in one of my proudest achievements.

Lion Brand Yarn

Like many knitters and crocheters, my first-ever project was using Lion Brand Thick & Quick, and it's still a favorite of mine to this day. So many of my all-time favorite yarns lines belong to you. I have loved working together over the last few years and getting the opportunity to design beautiful things with your yarn. I look forward to seeing what other work we collaborate on. Lion Brand is my weakness—my house is already filled with your yarn and it's still not enough. Thank you for generously contributing your beautiful yarn for this book.

WeCrochet

As the collaborator in my first true large-scale collaboration with a yarn company, WeCrochet has a special place in my heart. It was such a wonderful experience to design our 2020 summer collection: Cool Crochet for Warm Days, where I really got a taste of what it's like to put together a truly comprehensive pattern. Thank you for taking a chance on me. Everyone I've had the pleasure of talking to from WeCrochet is kind, helpful and encouraging. You are one of my all-time favorite yarn companies, and it is truly an honor to have the opportunity to use some of my favorite yarns in this book. I'm so grateful to have connected with Sara and Heather, who always go above and beyond to sing my praises and offer support. Sara, I hope to someday have as many beautiful fingering weight sweaters as you do. I truly love WeCrochet yarns so much and will never stop using them.

LoveCrafts

Thank you LoveCrafts for generously providing yarn for this book. The wide range of brands you carry, from big box yarns to indie dyed, makes you the ultimate one-stop-shop for any crocheter, for any project. There are so many yarns I've tried over the years that I probably wouldn't have otherwise had the chance to use if it weren't for your extensive line of products. Thank you for spotlighting me in 2020 for Indie June and recognizing the importance of size-inclusive design! I am so grateful to have the chance to collaborate with you.

The Hook Nook

Jessica, it has been such an incredible experience watching the process of your book coming together as I was just starting to write mine. The crochet community is so lucky to have you in it. You are such a wonderful human and an incredible storyteller with a powerful voice. Your brand is so distinguishable, so uniquely Jessica. Watching your product line come to life and getting to use your yarns in this book was such an honor. Thank you!

About the Author

Janine is an independent knit and crochet designer from Winnipeg, Canada.

She learned to knit and crochet in 2016 and has been designing patterns full-time since 2017. In addition to independent designs, Janine does freelance design work for a range of yarn companies and has quickly gained recognition in the crochet industry for creating modern, wearable sweaters with an inclusive range of sizes. She lives with her partner, Matt, and their two huskies, Pancake and Joe. She is a lover of fashion, interior design, plants, DIY and all things creative.

Her 5-piece summer collection, Cool Crochet for Warm Days: A Knits 'N Knots Collection, a magazine-style publication, is available on crochet.com. Janine also contributed to *Our Maker Life: Knit and Crochet Patterns, Inspiration, and Tales from the Creative Community.*

Modern Crochet Sweaters is her first book.

Her website is knitsnknots.ca.

Index